we two Alone

Attack and Rescue in the Congo

Ruth Hege

EMERALD HOUSE

BELFAST
NORTHERN IRELAND  GREENVILLE
SOUTH CAROLINA

We Two Alone
Attack and Rescue in the Congo

Published by

Emerald House Group, Inc.
1 Chick Springs Road, Suite 206
Greenville, SC 29609 USA

and

Ambassador Productions
16 Hillview Avenue
Belfast, Northern Ireland
BT5 6JH

ISBN 1-889893-22-6

Cover design by Matt Donovan

To

Mr. and Mrs. Ernest Ferrel,
who willingly gave their beloved
daughters, Winifred and Irene,
to the Lord to live or to die
confident that
whether they live or die
they are the Lord's

Foreword

The author of *We Two Alone* was a valued member of Baptist Mid-Missions for twenty-seven of the thirty-two years of her missionary labors in Congo and then Venezuela. Through her ministry across this land the Spirit of God was pleased to move young and older alike to dedicate themselves for Christian service. Since the fiery experiences of that last week in January 1964, lives were touched and attitudes changed as she bore again and again a quiet testimony to the faithfulness of our omnipotent God.

Miss Hege suddenly found herself catapulted into the world spotlight through her harrowing four-day pursuit and her companion's murder by the *Jeunesse,* a Communist-trained youth organization of Congo. Their tactics, God's wonderful deliverance, and Miss Hege's vivid account of her reactions, combine to make an intensely interesting story of modern missions in the face of extreme difficulty. This vital addition to the field of contemporary missionary literature has come in response to the leading of her great Deliverer and the urging of many friends.

The reader is impressed with the importance of an up-to-date, vibrant faith in an all sufficient, all-powerful God. He stands by in mute silence as he beholds just a glimpse of the intimate exchange between the loved and her Beloved.

We Two Alone is the story of the dynamic faith of two single women missionaries dedicated to carrying out Christ's commission to take the gospel to those still in darkness and sin. The reader will thrill to read of Miss Hege's witness to her captor as he stood over her with bow and arrow threateningly drawn.

It will be the rare reader who will put this book down until he has read the entire account. Though it is not fiction, these facts, born out of the crucible of human experience, read like fiction yet give us an insight into the purpose, problems, and pathos of modern missionary endeavor.

Allan E. Lewis DD,
President Emeritus
Baptist Mid-Missions
Box 308011
Cleveland, OH 44130-8011

Preface

An ebony backdrop of man's utter extremity and helplessness is required to adequately display the many sparkling facets of God's exceeding great faithfulness. My days in the hands of the Congo terrorists were one long testimony to the fidelity of my loving Heavenly Father. That the Lord wrought a mighty deliverance is indisputable and that deliverance stands as a fresh revelation of the power of united prayer. I am alive today to write this story only because the secret, invisible "telephone" which my assailants sought so diligently was constantly in use as prayer was made without ceasing. I gratefully own my indebtedness to all who prayed for my safety and rescue.

Viewing my experiences of those four days among the terrorists from the vantage point of retrospect, I am filled with a sense of awe and wonder that I should be the one chosen of God to be the object of such manifestations of His love and power and faithfulness. When I realize that one as unworthy as I has been entrusted as a steward of these difficult but exceedingly precious experiences, I can only marvel at God's grace. It is required of a steward that he be faithful in distribution of *all* that God has given him. As His steward I dare not hold these spiritual treasures selfishly, but share them for the enrichment and encouragement of all who will read.

On the other hand, I confess to a certain reluctance to record in black and white such intimate, personal episodes for the perusal of a public, oftimes curious and unsympathetic or even severely critical of simple faith in an all-powerful, prayer-hearing, prayer-answering God. It was at the persistent exhortation of friends and the gentle urging of the Holy Spirit Himself that I have written this simple narration of facts—a task for which I have felt most inadequate.

With sincere gratitude I acknowledge the prayer support of many friends concerning the preparation of this manuscript. Those of us who have worked together to produce this testimony have been very conscious of the strong succor of their intercession. Therefore, if there be any praise or honor let ALL of it go to Him Who has drawn near and worked with us. He, alone, is worthy of all praise and glory.

Helen Mary Sees, in her poem "Obedience," * so well expresses my feelings about writing this book—

> Lord, Thou hast given me this task,
> And I have not the skill,
> But Thou desirest of me, Lord,
> Obedience to Thy will.
>
> And so I give to Thee my hands,
> My mind and heart are Thine;
> Thou wilt supply the lack in me,
> Thy wisdom will be mine.
>
> Thou hast a purpose for this work,
> And this one thing I know,
> That Thou wilt bless it to Thy use
> When I obedience show.

* Published in *Moody Monthly* (Feb. 1964). Used by permission.

Acknowledgments

I am deeply grateful for the blessed, though somewhat poignant, nine days spent on the Ferrel farm in Jerome, Idaho, where the members of the family unstintingly gave of their time to reminisce and share with me the highlights of Irene's childhood and youth. Most of the letters Irene wrote to her parents during her years in Congo had been preserved and these were made available to me. Sincere thanks go to Miss Wyla Weekley and others for help in sorting and collecting usable material from the piles of correspondence.

To those who so effectively and graciously helped in the preparation of the manuscript I am profoundly indebted—to Mrs. Katharine Boerwinkle for her willing and invaluable aid in the writing of the rough draft; to Mrs. Doris Heflinger for her arduous and persevering labor at the typewriter; to Miss Mary Thompson for her constant encouragement in the arrangement of the final manuscript and her diligent, painstaking labor expended on the maps.

Credit is due Dr. Ray Bartholomew for his helpful suggestions in the initial outline of the book and in giving time to read the manuscript.

A heartfelt thanks to all of my fellow missionaries in Congo for their constant and hearty support in this undertaking. Many helped by contributing valuable material for which I have sought to give due credit in writing the book.

I would be most ungrateful if I failed here to acknowledge the loving hospitality of my sister and brother-in-law,

Lydia and Kenneth Avery, in opening their home to me not only for my base of operations while in the States, but in providing a quiet "prophet's chamber" in which to work. And, last of all, for the help and inspiration of that host of unseen friends and family who made the publication of this testimony to God's faithfulness possible, I am deeply thankful.

Ruth Hege
Wellington, Ohio
September 1964

I
In the Eye of the Storm

*For thou hast been . . . a refuge from the
storm, a shadow from the heat, when the
blast of the terrible ones is as a storm against
the wall.*

Isaiah 25:4

It was Friday afternoon, January 24, 1964. We were standing in the shade in front of our house in earnest conversation with the primary school teachers. They were facing the necessity of closing school. Nkedi, the director, was the spokesman:

"We fear the beating of the drum [the Congo school bell] for classes is inciting the *Jeunesse*. Already they have forced the closing of the village schools. We are not cowards, Mademoiselle,"—the fact that they had continued the daily schedule of classes until that very hour, even in the face of threats, verified the truth of his statement—"but neither do we want to endanger the children and the entire work of the station by ignoring these ominous signs."

The anxious faces of the teachers portrayed their concern.

"We hear of schoolhouses being burned, and of teachers being beaten and mistreated. Would it not be best to give the children a two weeks' vacation until things get back to normal?"

Our station had been remarkably quiet and peaceful. In the periphery of villages about us we knew there were hostilities and insurrection. But we were as the eye of the hurricane, untroubled and undisturbed by the gathering clouds. Missionaries and Congolese pastors who had recently visited us had noted and remarked about the unusual atmosphere of calm and quiescence.

The whirring of a plane immediately above interrupted our conversation.

"*Avion! Avion! Avion!*"

From every corner of the compound we heard the cries of excited people running together. We looked up and saw the little red and white MAF (Missionary Aviation

Fellowship) Cessna flying low over the station. The pilot tossed an object with a trail of white bandage which fell into the bushes behind the house. Everyone scampered for it. Timothy, our houseboy, reached the spot first. Hastily he untangled the bandage from the bushes. We ran to meet him. Irene's fingers trembled as she tore the bandage from the Gospel of John. Tucked inside she found a note which we read together:

> Are you in trouble? All missionaries have been evacuated from Mukedi. Kandala Station burned and missionaries evacuated.
>
> If everything is O.K. and you want to remain on your station, stand with your hands at your side.
>
> If there are signs of trouble, and you plan to drive out, wave your hands above your head.
>
> If you want to be evacuated, sit on the ground. We will send a helicopter for you.

The startling news of Mukedi and Kandala made us realize the seriousness of the situation. We knew the note demanded an immediate decision. Noisy talking and loud discussions filled the air. The girls, crying hysterically, clung to Irene. We, too, were in tears. Our orderly mission station of a few minutes before was now the scene of confusion and near bedlam.

The little plane circled the second time. We must signal our answer.

"Lord, lead us," we prayed from fervent hearts.

Hand in hand we walked into the clearing in front of the house and sat down. The Cessna tilted, dipped one wing low—their signal that they had received our message. It straightened, soared into the air, and moments later disappeared into the northeast.

A plane, or *ndeke* (bird) as it was frequently called by the Congolese, was nothing new or strange to us out on our bush station of Mangungu. Almost daily and often many times a day we heard the humming of the engines of the large transport planes, carrying their cargo of passengers or supplies to other parts of Congo. Sometimes even a jet would leave its cloudy trail in the clear sky. We often wondered, as we looked up at the large silver *bandeke* (birds) roaring through the heavens, if they were even aware of our little mission station tucked on the side of the hill in the midst of the Congo bush.

Yes, we were used to planes occupied with the affairs of the big world outside, but never before had one come with a message just for us. We realized that the vague uneasiness, which had for the last few days permeated the atmosphere of our otherwise peaceful mission compound, was not without grounds. The *Jeunesse* (French for "youth") evidently was closing in upon us. Now we would have to leave the place which had become so much a part of our lives and the people who had become dear to us. To them, under God, we had given ourselves to become their "servants for Jesus' sake." And now we were so suddenly to be taken from them.

I looked around at our beloved Congolese friends, now a noisy, chattering throng. There was Luka the pastor, and Benoit the Bible School teacher, and Gaston the male nurse, Akiem the watchman, the primary school teachers, the school children, the Bible School students, the workmen and the women from the compound, and the patients from the hospital huts. All were talking excitedly in little groups.

Glancing from one anxious face to another, I had a moment of misgiving. Did we do the right thing in giving the signal for evacuation? Should we have stuck it out with our native Christians? Was it right to leave them alone when the storm clouds were moving this way? The breaking fury of the storm now seemed imminent. Neighboring missions had already been attacked. Would we be next? There was no time to lose. My watch showed three o'clock. The helicopter would be coming for us within a few hours and there was much to be done. The Lord would lead us aright; He would not let us lose His chosen way, and would do that which was best both for us and for those who had come to know Him as Savior. We would prepare for evacuation, and if He had other plans, He could and would still overrule. With misty eyes, I turned and walked quickly into the house.

The situation in which we found ourselves did not develop overnight. Ever since Congo had declared her independence from Belgium on June 30, 1960, there had been a growing feeling of discontent. Cunning Congolese politicians had promised their people sudden and miraculous promotion to the same places of authority and wealth that their white leaders formerly held. They said there would be no more taxes, no more hard labor in the fields for the women; there would be secondary schools in every village, paved roads, large homes, bicycles, automobiles, and an abundance of food and clothing for everyone. This was to be all theirs overnight ushered in on June 30, by that most desirable, intangible thing called "Independence." No work, no responsibility, no struggle, just independence.

It was even rumored that their dead ancestors would be raised and would bring with them truckloads of money. The women were ordered to clear wide paths to the village graveyards so that the resurrected dead with all their riches could drive to their homes unhindered.

And then overnight they were catapulted into "independence." In less than a year, the reality of "independence" had become a bitter, distressing disappointment. Instead of the promised Utopia, there came economic collapse, intertribal warfare, unemployment, graft, bribery, an undisciplined army, and a wavering, unstable government. Resentment against political leaders and government officials ran deep.

"When is this independence going to end?"

"Let's give independence back to Belgium."

"The Belgians never treated us unjustly like our own people are treating us."

Questions and pathetic complaints such as these epitomized the feelings of our poor, disenchanted bush folks. When the fact dawned upon them that independence had come to stay, they accepted it with a kind of helpless resignation that bordered on despair. Cloth, matches, salt, soap, and other necessities of life were becoming increasingly hard to get, and prices on these items (when obtainable) were soaring far above wages. The stage was set for communism to exploit the situation to its fullest.

Peking-trained Mulele Pierre gathered groups of disillusioned, insurgent *Jeunesse* into forest hideouts where they were indoctrinated and trained in the art of guerrilla warfare. Reports had it that "the rebel warrior carries one knife, one bow, and one arrow, which they say will kill nine men. He receives one 'injection' of antibullet serum plus an overdose of ego-inflating lies. With these he is equipped to murder unarmed government employees, terrorize the general populace, and mistreat missionaries."

Mulele's village was some thirty miles from our Mangungu station. In late September we heard the news that soldiers had been sent to capture Mulele. The wild and extravagant story that the bullets shot at him turned to water and fell harmless to the ground was vouched for and firmly believed by his adherents. Later there were harrowing accounts of murders committed by the *Jeunesse* under the cover of darkness—a village chief to the east of us, a school director to the west, were dragged from their houses, beaten and hacked to death. Word reached us of bridges destroyed, trucks burned, deep trenches dug across the roads, government officials fleeing their posts. There were many conflicting reports. Knowing the Congolese relish a good story, we wondered how much was fact and how much was fiction.

We were thankful for the peaceful and relaxed atmosphere that characterized our station. Daily activities continued: primary school, Bible School, medical work, the building of a sun-dried brick house for Pastor Luka, village women coming to sell their produce. We were conscious of the overshadowing of the Almighty: "A thousand shall fall at thy side, and ten thousand at thy right hand; but it shall not come nigh thee." Psalm 91:7.

Then the central government sent in Congolese soldiers to hunt out Mulele and his followers to deliver them, dead or alive. The undisciplined army, lacking supplies from the state, foraged for themselves. Their plundering, pillaging, and raping terrorized the villagers. One day as Irene and I traveled along nearing a village we saw a number of uniformed men chasing a fat, female goat across the road. They were shouting orders to the villagers to help them catch it. Men and women stood watching, helpless and bewildered. Such an animal spelled wealth to its owner, probably all he possessed. Doubtless he had fattened it for sale at the market to buy clothing for his family. I am certain that the goat went into the pot for the soldiers' "chow" that night and the owner was left without remuneration.

Christians from the villages came secretly, under cover

of darkness, carrying tin trunks, boxes, and bundles on their heads, bringing their *treasures* to the mission for safekeeping. They had so little—only the bare necessities of life— a few plates and cups, a kettle, a pan, a shirt, a pair of sandals, a mirror, a few yards of cloth—these are the items that comprised their worldly treasures. Now even these trivial commodities had to be guarded from the marauding army.

Young girls ran to the mission for protection. We took them in. At once Pastor Luka sent out a call to the village chiefs to send in grass and bamboo (Congo building materials). Shortly a house was ready for the girls, within sight of Irene's bedroom window. Every night she had devotions with them and their lusty singing of Gospel songs echoed throughout the compound. Their merry laughter floated across the station as they kicked a ball by moonlight or sat around the fire relating their *bingana* (fables) or listening to Rosalie, the wife of their *kapita* (caretaker) spinning one of her imaginary yarns for their amusement before counting heads and sending them off to bed. All thought of danger was dismissed.

The soldiers set up roadblocks, making traveling difficult. It was hard to get anyone to go for our mail. Frequently young men were stopped, relieved of their possessions, and beaten before they were released to go on their way.

Truly our hearts went out in sympathy to the village people, though for ourselves we felt there was nothing to fear. We still could travel freely. On our previous evangelistic trips we had visited the soldiers' camp in Idiofa a number of times with the local pastor, calling in the homes of the professing Christians. They knew us and our little Volkswagen and usually removed the roadblocks without question, as they waved us on with a smile.

Ntshene Gaston, the nurse, with his family was coming to take over the responsibilities of the dispensary. He was delayed for several weeks because of destroyed bridges and roadblocks. On December 11 when the bridges were repaired, Irene went to get him. It was music to our ears when the little VW came chugging in late that night, fairly bulging with its cargo of six children and three adults, all safe and sound. The little family was thankful to be again within the protective confines of the Mangungu station. Gratefully they relaxed.

Neither were Christmas festivities on the station hampered by any warning of impending peril. The program, depicting the birth of the Savior by appropriate Scripture and Hymns, was well attended by the local chiefs and their people. The feast for the Bible school students and their families on our back patio proved to be a joyous occasion. Our outdoor "Christmas tree" was a natural grove of palm trees, gaily decorated with clusters of purple bougainvillaea. The large classroom desks, arranged in a circle and each marked with a "place card" in large chalked letters, served as individual family tables. In the center of the circle stood our aluminum folding table bearing huge kettles of steaming food, from which Timothy and Philip ladled generous servings of highly seasoned goat meat and rice on the extended plates of the smiling guests as they marched by in single file. Christmas cookies with coffee for the adults and milk for the children made the final course of the feast. Then appropriate gifts were distributed to all present and for the grand finale Irene played the folding organ while we joined in a carol sing. Happy voices rang out across the compound . . . "O come, let us adore Him, Christ our King."

After the holiday celebrations at Mangungu, Irene and I spent two weeks of vacation with fellow missionaries on other stations. We returned refreshed in body and spirit, content again to take up the work the Lord had given us to do. We knew that He Who had helped us *hitherto* would *henceforth* be our Guide. In a letter from Mangungu on January 9, 1964, I quoted two verses from a hymn * expressing our sentiments as we entered the New Year:

"We rest on Thee"—our Shield and our Defender!
We go not forth alone against the foe;
Strong in Thy strength, safe in Thy keeping tender,
"We rest on Thee, and in Thy name we go."

"We go" in faith, our own great weakness feeling,
And needing more each day Thy grace to know:
Yet from our hearts a song of triumph pealing;
"We rest on Thee, and in Thy name we go."
                                              —Edith G. Cherry.

For some time I had suffered a nagging toothache. On the weekend of January 11, Irene and I drove to Kikwit, the capital of Kwilu Province and our supply center. After having been without a dentist for over two years, we were thankful for Dr. Peters of the Mennonite Mission who had set up his office in Kikwit some two months previously. The abscessed tooth was extracted, a few necessary purchases were made, and we hurried back to spend Sunday with our fellow missionaries at Iwungu where Irene's sister and her husband, Winifred and Bob Grings, were stationed. Iwungu, just midway between our station and Kikwit, made a convenient stopping point to break the tedious four-hour trip.

That Sunday was one of special joy and significance.

* "We Rest on Thee," in *Hymns* (Chicago, Ill.: Inter-Varsity Press, 1947).

Several of Irene's closest friends from the station where she had worked previously were there, Bob Grings's sister and family (the Darrell Champlins), and his brother Mark. Winifred, with Irene's assistance, had prepared a chicken dinner with all the trimmings for our crowd of twenty-two. There was much good homey, cheerful missionary conversation about gardens, roads, children, chickens, and churches. After the dishes were done we all gathered around for a hymn sing with Irene at the piano. The tape recorder was brought out and she played the hymn "Face to Face" * for her parents in Jerome, Idaho.

> Face to face with Christ, my Savior,
> Face to face—what will it be?
> When with rapture I behold Him,
> Jesus Christ who died for me.
>
> What rejoicing in His presence,
> When are banished grief and pain;
> When the crooked ways are straightened,
> And the dark things shall be plain.
>
> *Chorus:* Face to face I shall behold Him,
> Far beyond the starry sky;
> Face to face in all His glory,
> I shall see Him by and by!
> —Mrs. Frank A. Breck.

Irene and I had planned to return to Mangungu that afternoon, but when the time came to leave, she was somehow reluctant to go. Did Irene have a premonition that this might be the last meeting with any of her own family? Or was she loath to leave the security afforded by the presence of so many missionaries—four men and seven women—to

* In *Inspiring Hymns* (Wheaton, Ill.: Singspiration, 1951).

return to a station where we two would be alone? We
decided to wait and get an early start the next morning.
How reassuring were the words in *Daily Light* for Monday
morning, January 13:

> Thou wilt keep Him in perfect PEACE, whose mind
> is stayed on Thee.—I will trust and not be afraid: for
> the Lord JEHOVAH is my strength and my song.—
> Why are ye fearful, O ye of little faith?—Be careful
> for nothing; but in everything by prayer and suppli-
> cation with thanksgiving let your requests be made
> known unto God. And the PEACE of God, which
> passeth all understanding, shall keep your hearts and
> minds through Christ Jesus.—PEACE I leave with you,
> My PEACE I give unto you: not as the world giveth
> give I unto you.—Let not your heart be troubled,
> neither let it be afraid.

We left with confidence and assurance. Not once were
we stopped. Surely the Lord was with us.

Busy days followed at Mangungu. It was the end of the
semester for the Bible School. Examinations had to be cor-
rected and grades recorded. Irene wrote to her parents on
January 21:

> I want to go to Idiofa on Thursday. I need to get
> some school supplies (notebooks, pencils, ink, slates,
> etc.) I will look for soap and various things for the
> natives. Also I want to get my driver's license renewed
> [the new post-independence law for chauffeurs re-
> quired that this be done every two or three months].
> . . . We have a Bible School fellow working on a new
> garden. Winifred shared her seeds with me. It is sort
> of dry now. A big rain came day-before-yesterday

and a child in our second grade in Luembe was struck dead. They brought him here for burial yesterday evening. I felt bad about it since no one seemed to know if he was saved. He has heard the Word of God every day in class. I hope it stirs the teachers to realize their responsibility to the children and to make personal contact with each of the children and know if they are saved. . . . I just finished a uniform for the nurse. I put a big pocket in it and a red cross on the yoke. I made one apron for Timothy and need to make another soon.

On Thursday, January 23, the day before the evacuation note was dropped from the MAF plane, Irene did go the twenty-five miles to Idiofa as she had planned. However, because the *Jeunesse* had destroyed a bridge and dug trenches across the one good road, she had to take an alternate route. That evening when she returned and told me about the work of the rebels, we decided that it would be well to make preparations to be air-lifted if necessary.

But Friday was so busy with school duties that even though we were aware of these developments little thought was given to evacuation. However, the MAF note made it imperative that we prepare at once.

As I entered the house I wondered where I should begin. Would it be possible to be ready within a few hours? It wouldn't take the plane long to fly back to Kikwit and send the helicopter—perhaps only two hours. Surely this did not mean that we would be leaving permanently.

"We will be back," we told each other and our Congolese friends.

We would leave the key to the house with Pastor Luka, and Timothy could come in and clean up after we were gone. This would doubtless be like the evacuation in 1960 after independence. At that time I returned after a year's absence to find everything in my home as I left it. Perhaps we would not even have to leave the Congo; maybe just go to Kikwit or Leopoldville and wait until conditions were safe and back to normal. Such thoughts were encouraging and our spirits felt buoyed up.

Yes, we would leave the house as it was, but there were things that were imperative and had to be done before we could go. Workmen had to be paid, accounts had to be settled with Bible School students, medicines in the pharmacy had to be checked, and school supplies turned over to the teachers. We decided to hide the car in the palm branch shelter where the men were making sun-dried bricks for the pastor's new house. We gave the keys to Pastor Luka, who promised to take good care of our faithful little VW for us. We gave some of our things as farewell gifts to our Christians. Last of all there were suitcases to pack with our most essential and treasured belongings. We were glad for extra time to get these things done.

It was getting late and the helicopter had not yet arrived. Timothy, Luka, Gaston, Benoit, Akiem, the students, and some of the Christians from the village gathered in our living room for a little farewell service. We sensed the solemnity of the occasion as we encouraged and admonished one another from the Word of God. Someone read Psalm 91:

"He that dwelleth in the secret place of the most High shall abide under the shadow of the Almighty. . . . Thou shalt not be afraid of the terror by night; nor for the arrow that flieth by day. . . . For he shall give his angels charge over thee, to keep thee in all thy ways."

Irene took her place at the organ and we lifted our voices in song. It was a beautiful quiet moonlight night and the words of assurance and confidence carried out through the open windows and doors across the mission grounds. "God will take care of you . . . When dangers fierce your path assail, God will take care of you," and "Glory over yonder . . . When we meet in Glory we shall part no more," ending with "God be with you till we meet again . . . Put His arms unfailing round you . . . Smite death's threatening wave before you . . . Till we meet at Jesus' feet . . . God be with you till we meet again." Our heads bowed in prayer as Pastor Luka committed Irene and me into the Lord's keeping as well as those who were left behind. We added one last word of encouragement from Philippians 1:6,

"Being confident of this very thing, that he which hath begun a good work in you will perform it until the day of Jesus Christ." With this promise our dear Congolese brothers in Christ departed.

Pausing a moment at the door, Luka said, "When the helicopter comes, we will be right here. We are not going to our houses to sleep tonight." They must have had a premonition that danger was near, but as if to relieve us of any sense of alarm he added,

"We want to be here to see the *avion* come down." Nurse Gaston and student Philip were delegated to take up their vigil in the living room.

Irene and I went to our rooms to prepare for bed. I looked at my watch. It was midnight. Once again I checked for passport and identification papers. Everything was in order. I lowered the wick of the kerosene light and got into bed.

Sleep did not come readily for my thoughts were occupied with the events of the past hours. The promised helicopter had not come but surely tomorrow—no today, for it was already Saturday morning, January 25—they would come for us without fail. What a blessing it had been to have had time for those few moments of fellowship with our own people who had shared with us the Word of God and who, unknown to us, were so soon to share also in suffering for His name's sake. It was comforting to know that even now they were lingering near. How good just to lie there and rest in God's mercy and lovingkindness—

"For Thou hast been . . . a refuge. . . . " There was PEACE in the EYE OF THE STORM.

2

The Storm Breaks

> The Lord hath his way in the whirlwind
> and in the storm.
>
> Nahum 1:3

Yes, it was peaceful in the eye of the storm. But storms move along their given paths until their fury is spent.

Suddenly I realized we were surrounded. We were no longer the eye, but a weak and helpless target directly in the path of the storm. Without warning that peaceful silence had been broken by the frightening thud of running bare feet. It was an instantaneous rush as of frightened cattle in a stampede, quick and unexpected. From all directions they were converging on our house. I heard the sharp cries of Benoit, Luka, and the others who were patrolling the grounds. Anger, fear, warning were in their voices. Our Christian friends were loyally trying to protect us, but they had no chance in the advancing floodtide of thirty or forty marauders.

The next instant blood-curdling shrieks pierced the stillness with the simultaneous crash of shattering window panes in my room. I jumped from my bed and stood in the center of the room trembling like a frightened deer, pursued and trapped by the hunters. Terrified, I looked about for a way of escape. My heart pounded violently as if it would leap from within me. I was clothed only in my nightgown. I felt horribly exposed. And then I noticed with gratitude that the drapes were still drawn at my windows. I must get dressed quickly and find Irene.

Hurriedly I jerked on the slip, skirt, and blouse which lay on the chair. My hands shook so I could scarcely fasten the buttons on my blouse. That which seemed most unlikely on our mission station was actually happening. The fury of the storm was breaking—breaking on us. The *Jeunesse* were attacking. With increased frenzy the shrieks and splintering of glass continued. My thoughts were still for Irene. I must find her.

Snatching my shoes, I darted into the hall. Irene was just coming out of the bathroom, fully dressed. She had not yet been in bed. We looked at each other bewildered.

"What shall we do?"

"Where shall we hide?"

"Shall we lock ourselves in the bathroom?"

Our questions hung unanswered in mid-air as the angry, infuriated *Jeunesse* broke in upon us. Our two Congolese volunteers keeping watch were able to escape—Philip through the front door and Gaston through a broken window at the back of the house. The invaders confronted us, brandishing grass torches. They carried bows and arrows and threatened us with long flashing knives.

"*Bima! Bima! Bima!*" (Things! Things! Things! it means in Kituba language. I later learned that *Bima* also means Get out! in the Lingala.) Gladly would we get out and let them have all our things, if they would but spare our lives.

My shoes, a most desirable possession to a Congolese, were yanked roughly out of my hand. Shoving, pulling, shouting frantically, they dragged us through the hall and living room, out the front door. One of the bandits pushed me unmercifully hard in the back, thrusting me down the front stairs. Fortunately I caught my footing. Another grabbed at the belt of my heavy poplin skirt. The jerk at my garment was so violent it all but threw me to the ground; it was ripped in two and taken from me. With horror I felt hands clutching at my blouse, which was of much thinner material. Providentially it did not tear.

We were surrounded by half-naked, drug-crazed savages, whipped to a frenzy. Maddened, they couldn't seem to stop. They pulled and pushed, pulled and pushed us another fifty feet across the grass.

Where were they taking us?

What were they going to do with us?

Did they intend to torture us?

I felt grateful that Irene and I were still together. But as these questions flashed across my mind, I saw ahead of us in the moonlight the menacing black body of a terrorist. He turned to face us. Horror mounted as I saw him fling something at us. His arrow came hurtling at Irene and with terrific force plunged into the left side of her throat. She instinctively reached up and with her strong hands pulled it out. Blood literally gushed from the wound.

"I am finished," she gasped, took another step, and collapsed.

"Oh, Irene!" I cried and fell to the ground beside her. Vaguely I remember being dragged by the arm. The bodily abuse by our assailants, the tremendous emotional drain, and the feeling of faintness at the sight of blood flowing from Irene's wound, apparently caused me to slip into unconsciousness.

When I regained consciousness, I was lying on the ground on my left side close to Irene under the large shade trees in front of our house. Evidently we had been dragged from the path where we had fallen and placed side by side in this more secluded spot. At intervals big drops of water splashed on us. I thought it was raining, but it was only the dew falling from the sheltering trees. I was cold—so very cold—and trembling violently. The cries of the frenzied, drug-crazed mob still filled the air, together with the slashing and smashing of things in the house. The bandits shouted to one another in their tribal tongue, and I could distinguish the words:

"*Nzo nkanda* (schoolhouse), *nkisi, dispensaire* (medicine, dispensary), *camion* (car)." As they continued their sweeping invasion of the mission compound, I heard the sound of hacking in the Bible School building, and the splintering of wood in the direction of the dispensary.

Someone came running, then came to a halt near me. My eyes were closed but I could sense his evil presence and could hear his mutterings.

"*Fwa*" (dead), I heard him say. He came closer and leaning over me put his hand on my side as if to make sure that his verdict was correct. However, before that bandit's hand ever touched my body, which just the moment before had been shaking uncontrollably, God's hand had been laid on me so that the trembling ceased and I was perfectly quiet. I seemed to sense that the man remained standing by me. A second time he put his hand on my side. Again God's

The Storm Breaks • 37

hand held me calm and still—so still that the terrorist must have been completely satisfied that I was dead. Another came and brutally yanked out a lock of hair. (It is common superstition that hair taken from a dead body and worn as a fetish imparts strength to the wearer.) Strangely enough the pain did not make me wince. Then the fourth time one came to abuse the supposedly dead body, and again God

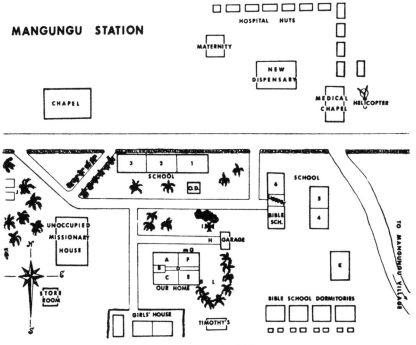

KEY TO MANGUNGU STATION MAP

(A)—Ruth's bedroom; (B)—bathroom; (C)—Irene's bedroom; (D)—Hallway; (E)—Kitchen; (F)—Living room; (G)—Steps; (H)—Irene felled; (I)—Left for dead; (J)—Missionary graves (Toma and Irene); (K)—Luka's unfinished house; (L)—Patio; (O.D.)—Old dispensary

gave perfect quietness. (Well do I know that it was only
His restraining hand that kept them from hacking our
bodies to pieces as they had done to three priests two nights
previously.) After the attacker went away, the trembling
started again, more violently than before. My teeth chattered from the cold and exposure. I prayed that my assailants would not return.

After a short time the whole mission compound was lit
up. They had set fire to the schoolhouse, probably with
their gasoline bombs, for the entire length of the building
was ablaze. There was more excited talking, then gradually
the voices died away in the distance and all became quiet.
Cautiously I raised myself on my elbow and looked around.
By the light of the burning building I could see objects
lying on the ground in front of our house. I supposed they
were dead bodies. I groaned in agony. I could feel cold,
sticky blood all along my left side and in my hair. I thought
it was Irene's. I reached out my right hand to touch hers.
It was stiff and clammy. Involuntarily deep moans of anguish escaped my lips. It was very cold and the scant
clothing left me was damp with dew and blood.

I saw the open door to our little bamboo, thatched-roof
garage. I marveled that they had not set fire to it. It would
be warmer in there. At least the dew would not fall on me.
But it would be heartless to leave Irene all alone outside. I
should keep vigil with her. The terrorists might return. But
I knew that Irene was no longer there; she was in her
Father's Home, forever out of reach of heinous torture. I
almost envied her.

Slowly and with much effort I got up and dragged myself over to the garage. By the light of the fire I noticed
two partially filled sacks of CPRA (Congo Protestant
Relief Association) foods. I spread out the cracked wheat
from the one on the discarded window shutter left there

by the carpenter and dumped the beans from the other sack in a heap on the floor. Closing the door, I lay down on the cracked wheat and huddled under the burlap sacks, which I covered over my chilled body. How thankful I was for this provision; soon my teeth stopped chattering and I became comfortably warm.

Through the cracks of the bamboo wall of the garage I watched the flames of the burning schoolhouse leap high into the air. Several times I thought I saw someone moving. Perhaps it was Pastor Luka or some of the Christians looking for us. On the other hand they too might be lying cold and lifeless under the stars. No, the movement was only the falling of a charred log. Apart from the crackling of the fire, there was a vast, aching silence. I longed to talk to Irene. What a faithful companion she had been to me!

Many years earlier, Irene had given her life to her Lord to do His bidding. Now her work on earth was finished and quickly, quietly, without suffering or anguish, the Lord had taken his faithful servant home. I could look beyond the cruelty of man to the will of an omnipotent, omniscient heavenly Father. I knew the arrow that felled Irene was not an accident in His plan. He was having *"His way in the whirlwind and in the storm"* and no terrorist arrow could mar His design.

Before Irene's birth the blueprint of her life was in the Master's hand and for more than forty-two years, with loving and patient assiduity, He had been building according to His pattern—an altogether perfect pattern, the completion of which led to a martyr's death and a martyr's crown. With joy He had seen His work completed. Her promotion day from earth to His presence had come in the early morning of January 25, 1964. It is written,

"Precious in the sight of the Lord is the death of his saints. . . . Blessed are they that die in the Lord, they shall rest from their labors and their works do follow them," and "Be thou faithful unto death, and I will give thee a crown of life."

I watched the fire burning itself out on the school-house. What a picture it was of Irene's life burning itself out for her Lord! How fitting the verse she quoted frequently during these last weeks together:

"For we know that when this tent we live in now is taken down—when we die and leave these bodies—we have a wonderful new home waiting for us up in heaven, a home that will be ours forevermore, made for us by God himself, and not by human hands." II Corinthians 5:1, *Living Letters.*

3
Girl of the Prairie

Therefore have I set my face like a flint.

Isaiah 50:7

The sturdy farmer reined in his galloping horse and stopped abruptly in the Johnson lane. It was past midnight December 18, 1921, near the town of Eagle Butte, South Dakota. Snow crunched beneath his heavy boots as he jumped off his mare, rushed up to the front door, and hammered loudly. The business that brought him out on such a night plainly required haste.

A man in nightshirt and carpet slippers, carrying a coal oil lamp, opened the door.

"Ernest! What brings you out on a night like this?" Mr. Johnson was conceivably surprised and concerned.

"It's Constance. She's in labor." The farmer's breath steamed the air.

"Well, you need help. Let me go at once to Dupree for Dr. Cramer. You go back and stay with your wife." Neighbors are indispensable on the prairie.

Back over the two miles to the little four-room frame house, where he had left the young mother in the throes of bringing their third child into the world, galloped Ernest Ferrel. As the minutes wore on, it became more and more evident that the doctor would not arrive in time to assist in the delivery. Dupree was twenty-three miles away; the country roads were bad; help could not be expected in less than two hours. But Constance Ferrel had carefully prepared all things in advance. There was no need for panic. Calmly she gave orders, which the anxious father carried out meticulously. When neighbor Johnson's Ford came chugging up to the Ferrel ranch, Dr. Cramer found a red-faced, blue-eyed baby girl, one of the chubbiest and kickingest he had ever seen, properly bathed and swaddled, lying beside a radiant mother. Moreover, Irene Elizabeth

Ferrel had already been committed to the Lord by her grateful, devout parents.

Fortunately for the energetic Irene, she was born and reared on the vast rolling prairies near the Cheyenne Indian Reservation. She expended some of her boundless vigor and zeal by riding Spark Plug bareback, and at breakneck speed, for miles and miles across the extended plains. She would grip her horse's mane, brake the gusts of wind with full face, let fly those blond tresses and, with shouts of unrestrained joy and exuberance, challenge her sister Winifred (fifteen months her senior) to a race.

In school she was conscientious; in athletics she was outstanding. Though her great love was softball, she outstripped all her classmates in any sport she entered. Her father, with unconcealed pride in his eyes, told me,

"In the county track meets she carried off most of the blue ribbons. When the dust cleared off the track, Irene was always found in the lead."

The same drive and energy characterized her even in hot, humid Africa. Over twenty years later she wrote from the Congo,

"You know me by now that if I have to sit in one place a long time I get restless and want to get away. Getting away for a day means a great deal to me." Another time she wrote, "Since I couldn't go to the village, I took my bicycle and went antelope hunting."

Not many young girls master the art of trapping, but Irene eagerly accompanied her older brother Dwight and learned from him how to set and inspect his traps. The prairie produced skunk, weasel, muskrat, and mink. With her own hunting knife she was taught to skin and dress their kill. Dwight admits today that his sister received very little monetary remuneration for her labors. His reasoning in those teenage days perhaps ran something like this:

"Irene is my apprentice; she is learning a good trade; she is fortunate to have me for a teacher." In addition the country was infested with rattlesnakes. The children became expert in killing them with sticks. It was their boast, corroborated by their father, that they never let one get away.

In time Irene's father granted her permission to handle a gun, again under the tutelage of Dwight. Having become an excellent markswoman by practice, she developed her shooting skill into a recreational hobby, one that accompanied her to the Congo. It was a useful hobby, frequently providing fresh meat of antelope, guinea fowl, or partridge for the missionary table; and monkey, large birds, or other animals for her Congolese friends.

The first year on the field she wrote from the station of Nkole Nkema,

> Last Tuesday was the eventful day I have been looking for as far as hunting is concerned. I went to the garden to see the plants and took my gun along. I walked on up the road toward our especially good hunting ground and saw an antelope feeding under a small tree. It was getting dark and I feared I could not see him through the sight on the gun, but the Lord helped me and I got him with the first shot.

In another letter she related,

> I came back with a nice female antelope which we dressed and put in the refrigerator. I got back to the road just as it was getting dark, tied the animal on the carrier of my bicycle and came along at a good rate. The Lord is good to give us meat thus. I saw the "*nse*" [antelope] from quite a distance and sneaked up

the road to come closer to her from another direction, the wind being the wrong way to approach her from the road. I got very close to her and was ready to shoot, when she smelled me and ran, but not knowing in what direction to run, she returned and came very close. I shot once and hit her, evidently in the stomach. Then I shot again after she had gone a few steps. The shot went through her heart and she soon slumped down. It seems a shame to kill them, yet how thankful we are that the Lord gives us meat thus. . . . Friday, when coming home from some villages I shot four birds: a bustard, a sort of stork pigeon, and two large hawks. We took the pigeon and bustard and gave the others to the Congolese pastors who were with us. They were so happy. . . .

Prairie life was busy but duties could be turned to fun and mischief when Dad wasn't looking. The pasture was in a lowland. Winifred and Irene had been assigned the responsibility of bringing up the cows in the late afternoon for milking. Why walk when one can ride, especially uphill? Experimenting, each grabbed a tail, and to their surprise two frightened cows bounded up the hill. This proved to be such fun that it called for a second run down the hill to catch two more unsuspecting victims. Their sudden fright and fast ascent made the journey all the more delightful. There was even time for a third try. In fact, thereafter, it was a real pleasure to go after the animals and several months elapsed before the Ferrels were again drinking milk from contented cows.

Nor were the pigs exempt from mischievous attention. Irene and Dwight had found a litter of little ones sound asleep against a wire mesh fence. The position of one of them was especially inviting. What would happen if they wrapped its tail around the fence and held on? A little skillful maneuvering accomplished this trick without disturbing its slumbers. Then, aroused by a vigorous poke, the squealing little shoat bounded off, leaving its tail behind him. Some time later, when the tailless hog was about to be slaughtered, the culprits confessed their misdeed to their father, who had been frankly puzzled about that freak in the litter.

Like most girls, Irene disliked washing dishes. She devised ways to evade the irksome task, in order to spend her time outdoors. On one occasion she went to the barn to help her father with the milking, leaving Winnie alone in the kitchen. It was dusk when she returned to the house. She could hear the rattling of pots and pans, knowing the job was about completed; she also could hear her sister singing lustily, probably to keep up her courage, for none of them wanted to be alone in the house when darkness came. In a moment she had an idea. She jumped up to the window and let out an eerie, weird noise. The effect was all she could have desired. There was a scream, a pot flew across the kitchen, and Winnie stood frozen on the spot with her hands grasping the air.

Pigs and cows notwithstanding, Irene was a lover of animals. Frequently when she was missing in the house, she might be found in the chicken coop sitting among her feathered friends, with one or two in her lap, fondly stroking them. Once, after a tornado tore the roof off the chicken house, her pet goose was nowhere to be found. Further search revealed that it had been trapped under the roof and crushed to death. It was an occasion for bitter, bitter tears.

She had better luck with her lamb. Lost from its mother, it had huddled in the ditch by the side of the road, forlorn and weak and almost dead from the cold. The Ferrel chil-

dren discovered it on their way home from fishing with
their father one spring day. Irene could look on only with
pity and longing for such a pet. She took it home, wrapped
it in a woolen cloth, laid it in a box by the kitchen stove,
fed it with a medicine dropper, and when it was a little
stronger, with a bottle. As she mothered it back to health,
it began to frisk and gambol about with such abandon that
even the old-timer, the big black-and-white shepherd dog,
Rover, gave it his attention. It wasn't long before the two
became fast friends and constant companions.

One can easily imagine that such a child as Irene was
willful and headstrong. However, having been reared in a
devout family, she respected and responded to her parents'
dealings with her, ready to confess her faults and make
things right when necessary. Her mother and father practiced the admonition in Proverbs 29:15,

"The rod and reproof give wisdom: but a child left to
himself bringeth his mother to shame."

Winifred recalls that their mother kept a switch above
the kitchen door to have it conveniently at hand when occasion demanded its application. Since Irene seemed to re-
quire the correction of the rod more frequently than the
other children, she surreptitiously disposed of it by throw-
ing it into the fire. Her victory was momentary and empty,
for the old switch was soon replaced by another, more
sturdy one, and the Scriptural discipline continued uninterrupted.

As her father remembered this incident, he reminisced a
little sadly,

"Yes, Irene did get the most whippings, but she probably needed them the most. But as we told you before, Irene
was always ready to acknowledge her wrongdoings and
seemed really sorry that she had been so impulsive."

How his cup must have run over when he read her birthday letter dated April 18, 1963.

> It is so good to have a Daddy that loves his children, as you do, no matter if we were disobedient and ornery (especially me, you know). I guess I have improved some, but have a long way to go! Thank the Lord for His patience and love and thank you for your love. May we walk pleasing unto the Lord thus being fruitful in every good word and work.

Family worship was an important part of the daily schedule of the Ferrel home. A chapter was read from the Bible, followed by prayer with all participating. Early in life the children were taught by precept and example to reverence the Scriptures as the inspired Word of God, to accept it without question as the final authority not only in doctrine, but in the business of practical daily living. Irene wrote just before she left for her first term on the field,

> You will never know what an influence you have had upon our lives. As I speak and give my testimony of my life, the one thing I like to bring home to people is the fact of a family altar as we had it. I am sure this was the greatest asset in many respects to keep us together as a family in the Lord and us children from going into the world.

Man's sin, his fall and subsequent lost condition, his need of salvation only through personal faith in the death of God's Son upon the cross of Calvary were thoroughly taught by the Ferrels and were accepted as fact without hesitation.

On one occasion in school, the discussion centered around the miracle of Christ when He cast out the demons called Legion and at their request gave them permission to enter into a herd of swine, which rushed headlong down the slope and were drowned in the sea. There was an attempt made to explain away the miracle and attribute the behavior of the pigs to natural causes. But so grounded in their faith and so sure of the truth of the Scriptures were the children that Dwight, as their spokesman, stood up as a young defender of the faith, insisting that he had lived on the farm all of his life and had never yet seen "one pig crazy enough to drown itself."

When Irene was nine years of age, Rev. Zook of Tabor College in Kansas came to the Congregational Church of Eagle Butte for revival meetings. During the week her sister Winifred became convicted of her sin. One morning as she stood at the scrubbing board helping her mother she confided,

"I would like to 'go forward' tonight. Do you think it will be all right to wear my tennis shoes because people will see them as I kneel at the altar?" Her mother gave assurance of her approval; she was certain also that God would approve.

Winnie heard very little of the words of the evangelist that night. Her mind dwelt on God, His Son Jesus, the One who said, "Suffer little children . . . to come unto me." She was conscious of her own failing. She sensed a dissatisfaction with herself she had never known before. There was somehow a strong attraction to the One she had learned about the long ten years of her life. He was not a vague, far-off something; He was a real Person; He was the Son of God. She knew He could make right all that was wrong in her life. Rev. Zook gave the altar call. Winnie sat frozen to her seat. What had seemed easy when she talked to her mother in the morning was impossible now. However, a gentle nudge from the maternal elbow at her side—and somehow it all seemed easy again.

The family remembers today that Irene too came under conviction of sin during that week. Her mother is no longer here to give all the facts, but from my close association with Irene I can understand what misery she experienced. Lacking the details, we can only guess at what must have transpired when she saw Winifred move out of the pew and walk down the aisle. She was happy for her sister; but she was unhappy. Instinctively she felt companionship slipping away. Winifred was the one she loved the most in all the world after Mother and Daddy, the one who slept in the same bed with her, the one with whom she whispered and giggled at night when they were supposed to be sleeping.

For a few days Irene was miserable. Spark Plug was recalcitrant; the cows were not much fun; she wished she could tie all the tails of all the pigs on the fence. She had the nagging impression that something ought to be done that had not been done. It was too much to bear by herself. She went to her mother and unburdened her heart. After a few encouraging words and the reminder of some Bible verses, Irene and her mother knelt together. In the simple words of a trusting child Irene told God the truth about her unhappiness; she confessed her sin; she asked Jesus Christ to come into her heart as Savior; she committed her life to Him as her parents had committed their baby girl nine years before. Fellowship with her sister was restored and joy was once again hers as she trapped and fished and milked and sat still at family devotions, and played with her little three-year-old sister, Ruth.

As a result of the revival meetings, fifteen souls were converted and formed their own Bible study group. About this time the South Dakota farmers were suffering repeated crop failures because of severe drought and plagues of grasshoppers. The lack of material gain, and sometimes of even the necessities of life, only spurred the little group to study the Word more earnestly. This resulted in increased faith and fuller trust in the Lord. They met one evening each week in the homes. Of this group Winnie says today,

"I will never forget those prayer meetings. What a source of spiritual encouragement to us young people! This is where we really grew spiritually. God was *real* to us. We saw many answers to definite prayer. We knew God heard prayer and had all power to answer. We knew God could do something about the rain so urgently needed, too."

One night the group agreed to pray for rain, and pray they did. Before the service ended, while petitions were still ascending, the sky clouded over and torrents of rain bathed and soaked the parched and thirsty land.

"Before they call, I will answer; and while they are yet speaking, I will hear." Isaiah 65:24. Prayer turned to praise.

A buoyancy permeated the air. Crops looked up, animals and people felt the freshness of the rain in their very spirits. Hope had been restored. It was almost like starting anew. Then the Ferrels remembered their baby turkeys. They hurried home from the prayer meeting half fearful of what they might find. They were not surprised, for everywhere lying about were rainsoaked, shivering, lonely turkey chicks. (Turkeys do not like rain. The young ones especially are subject to ailments and death when their feet get wet.) With a quick inaudible plea to Heaven the family gathered the skinny, drenched, ugly little birds, wiped off the excess water, and put them in tubs near the kitchen stove to dry. Their God again showed His hand; almost every one of them responded to the treatment and they were soon strutting around as lively as ever. The Ferrels have always counted this nothing less than a miracle.

The naturalness of prayer is gained by practice. From family altar, prayer meetings, Bible study groups, contact with other Christians, Irene learned to obey the Scriptural command, "Pray without ceasing." She wrote from the field on October 8, 1951,

> The Lord has been good to answer prayer for meat. Mr. Bell got an antelope last Tuesday and one Thursday, and they got three monkeys for the workers. We have been definitely praying for meat and it is one of the answers to prayer which we have had right along. We have a prayer list and pray for certain things each morning in our devotions, then put down the dates when we receive the answer. We prayed for rain Friday and Saturday since we hadn't had rain for a week. The Lord answered Saturday night and gave us a fine rain. It rained some Sunday but stopped in time for service.

When Irene was thirteen years of age the first great sorrow came into her life. Her mother had been ailing for some time, suffering from anemia. One morning the household awoke to find one side of her body paralyzed. She was taken immediately to the hospital at Pierre, some ninety miles away. Though she was given blood transfusions and the proper medication, she was by now too weak to respond to treatment. In less than a week the four children were left motherless. The rugged pioneer farmer stepped courageously into the breach and took the place of both mother and father to the family.

It was during the economically depressed thirties. South

Dakota continued to be held in the grip of the drought until it became impossible to get enough feed for the cattle. In the summer of 1936, a year after the family was left motherless, unable to sell his farm, Mr. Ferrel left it to move farther west. While he and Dwight were taking the cattle to Minnesota for sale, the three girls stayed in the home of a friend in the town of Eagle Butte. The strange couple, Rover and the lamb, had been left to guard the farm. Imagine the surprise and delight of the children the next morning when they opened the door to find their pets, Rover and the lamb. Like Mary's little lamb, the two had followed them the three and a half miles to town.

When the men returned and the truck was packed with the household goods for the move west, Mr. Ferrel announced that the dog was to be left behind. Irene protested. She clung to the dog.

"If Rover has to stay, I want to stay!"

Probably thinking of the wife and mother he was leaving behind, he appreciated Irene's need of her pet and gladly made a place for Rover on the truck.

The family settled in Filer, Idaho, where Winifred and Irene graduated from high school. This great event was matched by another: their father married again. Elsie Williams, a sister to Constance and much like her, stepped into the breach and took over the duties of wife and mother. The transition from aunt to mother was welcomed by all, and this new relationship proved to be a marvelous blessing to the entire family. Two years later, the youngest member of the family, Ruth, who by now was eleven and a radiant little Christian, died of a heart ailment.

The family's next and last move was then to Jerome, Idaho. Elsie, the new mother, was a graduate of the Bible Institute of Los Angeles (Biola). She did much to encourage the girls to further Bible training, helping them in every way possible. Concerning this, Irene said,

"I'm so happy for your spiritual help, Elsie, and your encouragement in our going to Bible school."

Both girls spent three years at Biola. Having chosen music as her major, Irene became proficient in piano, organ, and accordion. She graduated in 1944. Her musical talent was a joy and blessing to many in later years in the Congo.

After her graduation Irene joined Rev. and Mrs. True Maxfield of the Bread of Life Chapel in San Diego, California, who were ministering to service men in that city. Through their Christian center and their personal interest in the boys far from home, hundreds of soldiers and sailors found new life in Christ Jesus. The Maxfields had just lost their own daughter through death. The wound was still fresh when they were introduced to Irene, who was the same age as their daughter. She came as a gift of God and was received as their very own into their home and ministry. In turn, she reciprocated by entering wholeheartedly into all the filial duties and privileges and Christian ministry at the Bread of Life Chapel. The relationship was a happy source of joy and blessing to all three in the years that followed.

The Maxfields eagerly followed the activities of their "adopted" daughter in the Congo until Mrs. Maxfield's Homegoing in 1963. Then the lonely and bereaved pastor's weekly letters continued to encourage Irene. When the mail brought that final letter from him, she remarked,

"He seems so weak. I wonder if this may be the last."

Irene could not know that she herself would precede Pastor Maxfield to their heavenly home by just four days.

Since the time of her conversion, Winifred had her face set toward the Congo where her aunt, Mrs. Winifred

Urban, had previously served under the Africa Inland Mission. In the summer of 1948, at a Bible Conference at Big Bear, California, Irene too felt the call of God to the Congo. Both sisters spent a year at the Fundamental Bible School in Los Angeles, after which Winifred sailed for the Congo under the Fundamental World-Wide Mission in the spring of 1949. Then in the fall of 1951 the way was open for Irene to follow her sister to the land of His calling. She chose as her verse Isaiah 50:7:

"For the Lord God will help me; therefore shall I not be confounded: therefore have I set my face like a flint, and I know that I shall not be ashamed." The years that followed were to prove how truly she had set her face like a flint to do the will of the Lord.

Irene wrote to her parents before leaving for the field:

"I have wonderful parents who have a wonderful Lord."

On August 4, 1951 she, with two other young ladies who were going to the same field, embarked on the M/S *Houffaliza*, a Belgian freighter going from New York to Matadi, Africa. She continues her letter on board ship,

"The Lord has given real peace in leaving and I'm happy. So glad for parents like you who stand behind us in prayer."

On August 22 she adds:

By my clock which is Idaho time it is now 1:15 p.m. I keep good track of you folks in having a clock with your time. It is 8:15 here. It is now getting to the place where you are sleeping most of my day and I sleep most of yours. . . . I cannot explain the joy in my heart to know that we are so near to our destination, and how wonderful to be in His will and to be going for Him. It does sadden one's heart to see so many native villages and natives along the shore and to realize that perhaps few of them know our Savior.

Her boat docked at Matadi, at the mouth of the Congo River on August 25, just three weeks after leaving New York. There on the docks to welcome them was Mr. Benton Bell, a fellow missionary who had traveled the 875 miles from their interior jungle station to help the three ladies through the intricate formalities of customs. He had been waiting a week and the joy of meeting again, this time on Congo soil, was mutual. They traveled by truck over sandy, bumpy roads—all four of them riding in the cab—the back piled high with boxes and barrels of equipment.

It had been a long two years of separation for Irene and Winnie. One can well appreciate the delightful thrill and deep gratitude with which these two met at the Nkole Nkema Station. The realization of that reunion far exceeded the eager anticipation of their meeting. Immediately Irene entered into all the activities of the station—gardening, cooking, office work, hunting, and caring for the Bell children to give the tired parents time for a rest. Three hours a day were spent in the study of the Lingala language.

In December of that same year Winifred was married to Robert Grings, the son of missionary parents. Bob's consecrated mother paid the supreme price for faithful, sacrificial Christian service and lies buried in the Congo. Four of the Grings's children returned to that land as missionaries. The lives of the Gringses and Ferrels became inextricably linked. Bessie Grings was one of the trio who had come with Irene to the field in August.

As soon as Irene could speak the Lingala sufficiently well to give the Word of God, she and Bessie went out on village trips together. They traveled by bicycle with porters carrying the bedding and food, staying overnight in *ban-zambola* (government-erected houses for the convenience of traveling officials), or in homes of the villagers. This work she especially enjoyed. In a letter to her parents written from the village of Mayaya Moke she gives this description:

> Two little boys are standing outside the veranda shades, peering through as though they were looking at two monkeys in a cage! Curious people, and white-skinned people are a curiosity to them. Now they are a little closer and they will come as close as we will allow them. Poor folks, one does feel sorry to see them with little or no clothes, dirty and neglected. But if they will only receive the Good News we have to give them, they will one day be removed from this sinful world and be like the Lord Jesus. . . . As at home, it is easy to become busied with every-day tasks and neglect the more important. As Mary, we need to be continually occupied with the Lord's work and not be "cumbered about with much serving." Much work is awaiting our hands and we do long to do what we can to reach the unreached. . . . It is remarkable how the Lord gives daily strength and rest as we do His work.

From Ingundela came this report:

> We called for carriers last night after the service. Usually one need not expect them until 8 or 9 o'clock but they were ready to go before we got out of bed at 5:30. We rushed around and got things together by 6:15. It was a cool day for which we thank the Lord,

and another beautiful trip through the forest. We arrived at 9 a.m.—not such a long trip as we had expected. The people were glad to see us . . . they came with eggs and enormous pineapple; the largest we bought for 3 francs (6 cents). We are able to buy *plantens* (a sort of banana) a foot long, at six for one cent. I like them. . . . It is such a joy to give out the Word and teach youngsters verses which will remain with them. . . . They will hear my accordion for the first time which is quite an attraction.

Later when Irene went to the city of Luluabourg for a shopping trip she writes:

Luluabourg is a large city and has all the conveniences of life, but I am glad we can live simply and less expensive. I am willing to sacrifice a little for the sake of using our money for the furtherance of the Gospel. . . . We have our parents to thank for bringing us up to be saving, and it is especially important to be thus as a missionary.

She was *pleased* and thankful for the menus she could concoct, using the foods which were native to that land. In her letter of August 17, 1953 Irene says,

"We had Spanish rice made with dried antelope meat which Winifred and Bob brought from their Yalima trip, baked bananas, greens from the forest, *kwanga* (a sour native bread made from manioc flour cooked in banana leaves) and lemon pie."

Her bent for athletics and the out-of-doors notwithstanding, Irene was a born homemaker. Like most women, she longed for a home and family of her own. There were those of the opposite sex who recognized her worth and stability of character. Opportunities for marriage were not lacking. But each time, as she sought the Lord's will for her life, she was led to continue alone.

In writing to her parents of some of the problems and frustrations that face a missionary on the field, Irene says,

> I am feeling better than when I wrote you last week. Am thankful that the Lord encourages when we become discouraged and despair of life. Life in the Congo isn't easy for a single girl from the standpoint of getting lonesome. If it weren't for Bessie's friendship it would be extremely hard. I guess my particular makeup isn't a help to me. Bessie and I both have felt that such a work as this is much better carried on by married couples, but the Lord sent us out and I am sure He will and has already used us. There are many single girls working in Africa, in fact, I suppose that nearly one half of the missionaries are girls. Whatever He wants for my life, I want. Don't ever let anyone tell you that anyone can fit in as a missionary. The CREAM of Christians is needed to fit in on the field. It isn't an easy place.

She usually wore her long, light brown hair in a neat roll, low on the nape of her neck.

> Hair is a problem here. I have it braided today. I do not like it but I guess it doesn't matter too much. No need to look beautiful here, just neat, which I try to do. . . . The Lord is really undertaking in all the problems we face, and He will be Victor as we yield and put our trust in Him. *I love Africa and love the people.* Oh that we might win many more to Christ!

In 1955 while home on furlough, Irene, together with Bob and Winifred Grings, joined Baptist Mid-Missions. Before returning to the Congo she spent some time in Brussels, Belgium, studying French. Before leaving for her second term in the Congo she writes:

> I have enjoyed my stay in Brussels, though very different from America. I find it a real mission field too. The Lord has burdened my heart for this little country to pray for the raising up of missionaries to come here. Will you pray with me for Belgium, for the separated testimony which has begun here and for laborers? *God has called me to Congo* so I do not consider remaining here, but I cannot help seeing the need.

From the Rev. B. J. Berge, pastor of the Baptist Church in Brussels, came this tribute for the memorial service for Irene held in Cleveland, Ohio, March 20, 1964.

> We thank God for every remembrance of our departed sister. Quiet and unobtrusive, she went her way among us. From the very first day in Brussels she joined us in our little church and helped as she could. Whether distributing tracts, washing dishes or playing her accordion, she was *serving the Lord*.
>
> Missionaries are very different one from another. Some strike us by their brilliant minds and quick learning of French, others by their friendliness or spiritual experiences. Irene was just simply a mirror of Christ to us. . . . The Lord Jesus came among us as a servant to serve. She was of the same mind, and serving Him, manifested Christ. We were all the time very conscious that it was not she but Christ.

I quote from a letter written to Irene's parents by one who worked and roomed with her at Iwungu:

> Irene was a woman of great strength—strength that perhaps was not apparent to those who knew her superficially, those who saw only the shy, quiet exterior. She had great reserve of physical and spiritual strength. . . . As roomates we did not always agree; in fact we sometimes disagreed heartily and I soon sensed Irene's conviction and oneness of purpose. . . . How often since that time I have wished that she knew how much I respected her faithfulness to her beliefs. . . . When we went to Nkole Nkema for Bessie's wedding she showed me the little hut where she had once lived—windowless, floorless, ceilingless. "Right over there in that corner," she said, "I shot a big viper one night." All that night I huddled under the blanket, dozing rarely, while Irene slept peacefully beside me. She was not afraid. . . . She died as she lived; quietly, valiantly. Irene has joined the ranks of those martyred for the testimony of their Lord—and she shall walk with Him in white, for she is worthy.

Irene Ferrel, girl of the prairie, had set her face like a flint to do her Savior's will. Her body, felled by a rebel's arrow, lay stark and cold in the moonlight; her spirit released from the body, as a homing bird from its cage, had soared to her heavenly Home, there to join the chorus of loved ones who had gone before—her mother, her sister Ruth, Mrs. Maxfield, and myriads of others singing that new song saying:

"Thou art worthy, . . . for thou wast slain, and hast redeemed us to God by thy blood out of every kindred, and tongue, and people, and nation."

4
We Two Alone

Whether we live . . . or die, we are the Lord's.

Romans 14:8

My first meeting with Irene was in Brussels, Belgium, in the fall of 1957. I was brushing up on French before returning to the Congo, after an absence of twenty years, most of which had been spent in a Spanish-speaking country. Irene was returning to the States on sick leave. She had undergone major abdominal surgery on the field. The doctors had discovered a collapsed lung, and being uncertain of the cause, were sending her home for further medical attention. I met her at the airport and took her to my room for a rest between planes. She appeared thin and frail, with visible signs of physical suffering. I was impressed with the quietness and calmness with which she told of her sickness and faced the possibility of not returning to her adopted land and the people whom she loved.

I saw her next in the summer of 1959 when I was directing our missionary Guest House at Kikwit during the vacation months from Bible school. During her stay at home Irene had major chest surgery and after the months of convalescence in the home of her parents in Jerome, Idaho, she was given medical clearance to return to Congo. I met her at the airport in Kikwit. It was a joy to see her looking well and eager to return to her work. Missionaries and Congolese friends united in praise to God for the miracle He had worked in her body and for returning her to us.

Irene went to Iwungu where the Robert Grings family was stationed, to take over the direction of the primary school. She did not want to get into the teaching work on the station, feeling that her calling was rather to women's and children's work and to a village ministry. Yet there was a need that only she could fill at the time. She met the challenge and did the work well. The joy of being once more with her sister, Winifred, and of working with the girls on the station compensated, in part, for having to do a job for which she felt unprepared.

She wrote her parents,

> I have begun a girls' class. It is such a joy to have the girls here. They are living next door to me here in the school building because in the girls' dormitory I cannot watch them closely enough to see what goes on. If I am going to have girls, I want them where I can protect and care for them.

It was on June 30, 1960, that Congo declared her independence from Belgium. Though for weeks before the atmosphere had been tense and foreboding with free expressions of antiwhite sentiment, the day passed with unusual calmness. The independence ceremonies in Kikwit were attended with a feeling of good will toward blacks and whites alike. We relaxed and gave ourselves the more earnestly to plans and preparations for the future advance of the Gospel under the new government.

It was but a few days later when the storm broke with madness and fury in Leopoldville. The army mutinied against their white officers and seized the arsenal. Horrible atrocities were committed by the Congolese soldiers as the white population fled across the river to Brazzaville. Similar uprisings broke out in many cities across the Congo. The United States government then facilitated the evacuation of its citizens. All but one of our Baptist Mid-Missions missionaries were air-lifted from Kikwit. Bob Grings chose to stay with his Congolese brethren, going from station to station encouraging the Christians until other missionaries were returned to relieve him.

Prayerfully and anxiously we watched the happenings in

the independent Congo, always with the hope that we would be permitted to return to our work there. Before the year was ended several of our married couples went back, but our Mission Council felt that conditions were still unsafe for single women. We waited in the States until August of 1961 when permission was finally granted for our return. A few weeks later found me in the village of Mbongo, a guest in the home of Manuel and Esther and their four children. Manuel had graduated from our Bible school the year before. They cleared out a corner of their humble mud-house where I put up my cot. The mosquito net of heavy material afforded the privacy needed. I could sense the old racial barriers of pre-independence years go tumbling down as we read the Word of God, prayed together and moved among the villagers. When I accepted the invitation to eat *luku* (a thick mush made of manioc flour) and hot mushroom sauce with them, our *kintuadi* (fellowship) was complete.

I found that the Word of God could be spoken with more liberty and authority when sharing the lives of the village people and living next to their heartaches and joys. It seemed reasonable that we should go to them rather than have them come to us on our comfortable mission stations. How true are the words of the prophet Ezekiel when he says,

"And I sat where they sat, and remained there astonished." Ezekiel 3:15.

I, too, needed to sit where they sat and *remain* there longer than an hour on a Sunday afternoon if I would enter into their disappointments and sorrows; if I were willing to sense the oppression of dense spiritual darkness, sin and superstition of heathenism, and their fear of the unknown spirit world; if I would sympathize with the depth of their soul distress. My responsibility as one who had been "called of God" to this dark land was to give them the best news in the world, to tell them of the power of God to free them from the bondage of sin and Satan, that they might turn "from idols to serve the living and true God and wait for His Son from Heaven." To make that Good News acceptable to the Congolese, I must try to find common ground with them that I might by all means win some to Christ.

A month later Irene, who had been detained at home because of her passport, joined me. With the full approval and blessings of our fellow missionaries we set out on our first village trip together. A new sense of urgency characterized our work. We knew that it was only God's grace that had returned us to Congo and was giving us another opportunity to serve Him in that land of tension and turmoil. A premonition that our stay there might be short roused us with fresh determination to give ourselves more fully than ever before to the important task of making Christ known.

The little Volkswagen, which I had acquired in 1959, unlike most missionary vehicles had not been appropriated by the Congolese. Because it was impossible to purchase a carrier anywhere, Bob Grings used his ingenuity and made one for us. Irene was an experienced driver and an excellent packer. By tying cot beds and a folding table on top, she found a place inside for the remainder of our camping equipment, as well as Timothy, our faithful boy, who accompanied us on all our village trips. Irene's accordion was a big attraction. Whenever or wherever she played, groups of men, women, and children gathered. We taught them Gospel songs and portions from the Word of God.

Irene and I anticipated with pleasure our ministry together. Our lives seemed to complement each other; however, to say that we always agreed would be an untruth. Like most missionaries, we were individuals of strong convictions, both called of the Lord to do a definite work, and we sometimes disagreed heartily as to how it was to be done. But our differences were short-lived. We both were veterans with enough experience to realize that little irritations and personality clashes, if not recognized and rectified promptly, could soon build up a wall of separation between us, making our ministry together ineffective. I John 1:7 gave us the only solution.

"If we walk in the light, as he is in the light, we have fellowship one with another, and the blood of Jesus Christ his Son cleanseth us from all sin."

Every evening as we read the Word of God and prayed together, recognizing afresh our oneness in Christ for Whose sake we had forsaken all that was dearest to us in this earth, to follow Him in Congo, and Who had so clearly brought us together, little differences melted away —and how very little and trivial they seemed in the presence of THE LIGHT in Whom there is no darkness at all. As we knelt before Him confessing our failings, the precious blood that God's Son shed for us cleansed us from sin and restored fellowship. Contrary to the opinion of many, missionaries are by no means exempt from the frailties "that flesh is heir to." We are still sinful men and women, needing constant cleansing, even though we may be kept from known sin by the grace of Christ.

The following January I was asked to join the staff at the Bible Institute at Mangungu where I had taught before independence. Reluctant to give up the village work, we were able to work out an agreement whereby Irene and I spent four days a week teaching on the station. Then on Friday afternoons when the last class was finished, we packed the little VW and went to a neighboring village for the weekend, returning to Mangungu on Monday. This arrangement required careful planning of our schedule to give sufficient time to the duties and activities of the station, but it proved a real blessing and asset to our entire work.

Our national pastor, Luka, would send word in advance of our coming. Chiefs vied with one another for our visits and invariably we were received with enthusiasm by the humble village folks. Always a house was waiting for us, emptied of its occupants, the dirt floor swept and watered down to settle the dust, and the welcome mat was out—in this case, the beaming faces of the owners of the house. It was a special honor to have the white missionary occupy their home, even though it meant that they themselves must live in the much smaller cook house. With gratitude we accepted their hospitality. What if the rats and roaches did play tag on the floor, roof, and walls, occasionally shifting to hide-and-seek under our mosquito net when some corner had not been tucked in carefully?

Naked children, their parasite-laden tummies protruding, their white shiny teeth even and strong from the diet of calcium-loaded bugs and worms, held out dirty little hands,

"*Baka beto! Baka beto! Baka beto!*" (Take us!)

Young women dressed in gaily colored native cloth, sleeping babies tied to their backs with fuzzy little heads bobbing, talked noisily, shoving and laughing; shriveled, stooped, toothless grannies, their raffia loin cloths, stiff and odoriferous from numerous applications of palm fat, wrinkled, black faces beaming approval, greeted us:

"*Bana bis! Bana bis! Bana bis!*" (Our children!)

This was village life.

We felt at home among our Congolese friends. Faithfully we gave out the message of salvation through Jesus Christ, God's Son. Truly the Lord was calling out a people for Himself from each one of those villages. Little groups began meeting together for Bible reading and prayer. The chief of Kimpata village said,

"We have grown very cold in the things of the Lord. God has sent you to rekindle the fire."

We realized that we, too, needed a constant rekindling of the fire of God's love in our own hearts as we ministered to them.

In October of that year the missionary couple who had been directing the Bible school in Mangungu felt that their work in Congo was finished. They returned to the States, leaving Irene and me alone. Bible school was temporarily closed. We were reluctant to give up our village work, but more immediate needs of the station kept us busy. Bible classes with the school children, the teachers, and the native church filled our daily schedule. Every week we had one of our Congolese families in our home for a meal. Timothy knew the likes and capacity of his own people, and he cooked the foods that pleased them, both in kind and quantity. Frequently the deacons and elders from the two local churches met in our living room to pray and seek a Scriptural solution to their problems.

When Akiem, our night watchman, who had once been a slave to the potent African palm-wine, fell again into that temptation and was found out, he was called before the deacons and elders and severely reproved and admonished from the Word of God. It was at their suggestion that we laid him off work. His repentance was so genuine that after six months of probation he was reinstated to his former position, with the full approval of the church.

When one of the primary school teachers fell into sin and needed discipline; when a thief broke into our dispensary and got away with some of the valuable medicines; when we outgrew our little one-room thatched-roof dispensary and desperately needed a larger and more permanent one; when the need of reopening Bible school became urgent and no director seemed available—these were occasions for the elders and deacons of both churches to meet together in our living room to pray with us and seek the Lord's will in these problems. We were never disappointed, for sooner or later the answer came, often "above all that we had asked or thought."

Not infrequently Pastor Luka called for a day of prayer in the church when the needs were kept before the Lord all day long by the faithful of the congregation. These were times of spiritual refreshing when we saw the Lord's hand work mightily on our behalf. We were pleased and greatly encouraged to see the native church taking over responsibilities they had previously left to the missionary.

It was at the invitation of our local churches that Miss Susie Brucks, a Mennonite missionary nurse from a neighboring orphanage, came to our station to supervise a medical work. For several months Susie spent two or three days a week with us. Under her direction, with the help of Stephen, a Congolese male nurse, the medical work grew until a hundred or more were receiving treatment daily at our little dispensary. Each morning, before medicines were dispensed, the patients and their helpers met in the chapel to hear the Word of God in their own tribal tongue. We prayed for the healing of their souls as well as their bodies. Since we were no longer able to get out into the villages, the Lord was bringing the village people to us. We were grateful for these opportunities to make Christ known.

Our one-room dispensary was no longer adequate. The women were summoned and with their short-handled hoes they cleared the tall grass from a large area of land across the road leading to Mangungu village. Soon a dozen grass hospital huts were up to house the in-patients. At the same time work began on a new four-room cement block dispensary. Building materials were very difficult to get; we had no truck and no male missionary. How could this work ever be completed? We turned to the One who best knew our needs and knew too how to supply them. The church joined in prayer for this was their project as well as ours.

It was amazing to see how the materials for the dispensary came in as needed: cement, boards, roofing, hinges, nails, screws. All these things had become very scarce since independence, and yet were needful for putting up a permanent building. The Lord touched the heart of a merchant in Idiofa not only to sell us the cement, but also to deliver it to the mission without charge. Irene hauled the boards most urgently needed, tied to the carrier of the little VW; later, Mr. Eicher brought us a truckload of boards taken from the forests near Balaka. A friendly Catholic priest sold us enough metal roofing from his supply, and Bob Grings brought the nails and screws from Iwungu. The work continued without interruption under the supervision of Luka. Many were the notes of praise that ascended to our heavenly Father during those months. In August the new dispensary building was dedicated.

In September of 1963, with the help of a Congolese teacher, Ntshundu Benoit, and with the approval of our fellow missionaries, we reopened the Bible school on Mangungu station. Nineteen young men were accepted. All but six were from the neighboring villages where we had itinerated. Our hearts overflowed with praise to God as we envisioned the future—a local church in every village under the leadership of consecrated, trained Congolese. Then, should the missionaries have to leave again, the Lord's work would go on without interruption.

It was thus we had entered 1964 with confidence. True, WE TWO ALONE were the missionary staff. But the Lord had given abundant evidence of His presence and had blessed our efforts above all we had asked or thought, and God's leading in our lives had been clear and unmistakable. Then in the early morning of January 25 this was all abruptly changed. Could it be true that the body of Irene, my dear companion and fellow laborer, was now lying cold and blood-soaked outside in the night with dew from the big tree gently dripping upon her? The only sound was the crackling of the fire and the occasional falling of timber from the burning schoolhouse. I knew that Irene was "absent from the body, and present with the Lord." She had already heard the sweet voice of welcome from her Savior's lips,

"Well done, thou good and faithful servant . . . enter thou into the joy of thy Lord." For *her* all trials and conflicts and labors were forever ended. She had entered into her rest and I was left *alone*. I shivered and trembled under the burlap sack from physical cold and soul agony.

Alone? Ah, no. As if spoken audibly I heard these words, "I will never leave thee nor forsake thee." Some days earlier I had read in the Amplified New Testament,

"God himself has said, 'I will not in any way fail you nor give you up nor leave you without support. I will not, I will not, I will not in any degree leave you helpless, nor forsake nor let you down, nor relax my hold on you. Assuredly not!' So we take comfort and are encouraged and confidently and boldly say, The Lord is my Helper, I will not be seized with alarm—I will not fear or dread or be terrified. What can man do to me?" Hebrews 13:5, 6.

A strong unseen hand covered me and the warm sense of God's presence enveloped me. The trembling ceased. I became calm and quiet. *I was not alone!*

5
The Aftermath of the Storm

*I will mention the loving kindnesses of the
Lord, and the praises of the Lord, according
to all that the Lord hath bestowed on us . . .*
Isaiah 63:7

At last, after what seemed an interminable night, the welcome light of dawn dispelled the ominous darkness. I stretched my stiff, aching limbs and laboriously inched off my bed of cracked wheat. My hair felt matted and caked with blood. My blouse was stiff and dry. My left arm, however, was moist and warm. Pulling up my sleeve, I was surprised to find a deep gash on my upper left arm. At the same time I noticed that miraculously my blouse was not torn. So I too had been wounded, although I could not tell·when it had happened nor could I help wondering what had caused it. Was it a knife, an arrow, or a lance? (Later Gaston said it was an arrow.) Whatever the weapon, the wound had been kept clean and profuse bleeding had served to wash out any possible poison and contamination.

Wrapping one of the burlap sacks about my waist for a loin cloth, I opened the garage door and stepped out into the fresh morning air. All was quiet. No one was in sight. With great relief and gratitude I saw that the objects in front of the house were not dead bodies left from the devastating attack as I had supposed at night, but were pieces of broken furniture thrown from our living room. I walked over to where Irene lay. The blood was completely drained from her body. Her face was ghastly white with the pallor of death. Looking down at her, I stood motionless, my soul a turbulent, churning battleground. Irene murdered!

Why had the promised helicopter delayed so long in coming? Why had we not been taken to safety before this heinous and unnecessary cruelty? What a shock this would be to her parents and to Winnie! Why had she been taken? Why was I left?

77

The awful turmoil of my soul was only momentary. Quietly the Lord spoke to me as He did to the tempest on the Sea of Galilee, "Peace, be still." As then, so now, there was an unbelievable calm. I knew God would do nothing not perfectly loving and wise and good. I listened as He poured His healing balm into my soul,

"My child, all powers in heaven and earth and hell are under My control, and nothing can touch you beyond My permission. I make no mistakes. This thing is from Me. Trust Me to do that which is for your good and My glory. 'You do not understand now what I am doing, but you will understand later on.'"

I looked up to see Luka standing beside me, his dark eyes staring with horror.

"*Bau imene kufwa Mademoiselle*" (They have killed Miss).

"*Bau imene kufwa Mademoiselle*," he repeated over and over as if in a trance. Then Timothy came—that lovable, loyal Timothy, who was especially fond of Irene. He looked on, grief-stricken, too shocked to say a word. Then he suddenly disappeared, only to reappear a few minutes later with the sheet Irene had presented to him the evening before. He covered her lifeless body, mercifully hiding her from the gaze of those who by now were gathering in numbers. Quickly the word had spread from mouth to mouth by teacher, school children, and sympathetic villagers.

"*Bau imene kufwa Mademoiselle! Bau imene kufwa Mademoiselle!*" It was like a woeful dirge chanted by a Negro choir as each put his cupped hand over his mouth, slowly waving his head back and forth in sad, mournful contemplation.

"*Bau imene kufwa Mademoiselle! Bau imene kufwa Mademoiselle!*"

I must then have come out of a daze, for it suddenly occurred to me that there was nothing more I could do for my dear co-laborer than to bury her "earthly tent house," which she had so recently vacated. Turning to Luka I said, "See if you can find someone to make the coffin and dig the grave. We will bury her beside Toma." Missionary Archie Haller was known as Toma, the spiritual father of many of the older Christians at Mangungu. He had died of a tropical ailment some twenty years previously and lies buried under the palm trees in a quiet corner of the compound. To Timothy I said,

"Go into the house and see if you can find anything in which we can bury Mademoiselle."

Timothy returned a few minutes later with my house coat, which he handed to me saying,

"This is for you. Put it on. Everything else is gone. I will get one of Rebekah's [his wife's] dresses for Mademoiselle."

So absorbed had I been in my thoughts of Irene that I had forgotten my own appearance. How shocking I must have looked to my native friends, with blood-smeared face, blood-stained blouse, blood-caked hair, burlap loin cloth, barefooted. How good God was to spare me the house coat. Gratefully I put it on.

Together we carried Irene and laid her on a split-bamboo mat on the dirt floor of the garage. Tenderly we closed her eyes and mouth. Timothy brought water from the rain-barrel, and several of the Christian women helped me wash and clothe her in Rebekah's slip and dress. Truly this was a labor of love. Tears mingled with rain water; audible and inaudible groans of anguish betrayed our grief and loss. Timothy, standing at a distance, could do nought but sob, unashamed.

The large gaping wound in Irene's neck revealed that

a jugular vein had been severed. Again I praised the Lord that her death was not a long, lingering, painful one, but that in a matter of seconds after she was hit, she was with her Savior where "there shall be no more death, neither sorrow, nor crying, neither shall there be any more pain." Revelation 21:4.

Timothy, ever alert to do his utmost, meanwhile brought my cot bed, which had been overlooked by the plunderers. We wrapped her in a white bedspread, also left, and laid her on the cot. In the garage, our "boy" again disappeared, this time returning with the dress I had given Rebekah as a farewell gift the night before.

"Here take this; you will need it," he said simply. Then with a *"Bika mbote"* (Farewell), he was gone.

Dear, devoted Timothy! How well I remembered that first morning when he began work with us. To us he was God's gift in answer to prayer, for we desperately needed a houseboy. Though he came from a distant village he was no stranger to us, for he had already established his reputation among the missionaries for his constancy and dependability. However, to the chiefs and elders of Mangungu village he was a stranger and they resented the intrusion of an outsider working for us. They gathered in our back yard to *sala makalele* (make noise or a fuss). After some loud and long discussion they agreed to give Nkumangulu Timothy a trial as our boy. Very shortly, however, by his cheerful disposition and his ability to mind his own business, Timothy won them over. No longer considered a stranger, he was accepted among them as belonging to them.

For two years he had helped us in the house—washing, ironing, cleaning, cooking, baking, bartering with the village women at the back door, and checking the gas and oil in the car when we were going on a trip. He had become an integral part of our household. Even in our times of relaxation when on Saturday afternoons we drove out to some road off the beaten path and parked the car, Irene with her gun and Timothy with his bow and arrow stalked the plains in search of antelope and other game. Now he was fleeing to his village. Rebekah was soon to be delivered of their first child and he must get her to safety.

The six Bible school students who were not from the neighboring villages were in a hurry to leave, too. This was my opportunity to send a note out with them, but it would be difficult to write or read without my glasses. As I entered the house, destruction faced me from every side, but there on the bedside table, just where I had left them the night before, were my glasses! I found paper and pencil in my desk drawer and quickly wrote a note to Intschueme, the orphanage where Mrs. Archie Haller, her daughter Geneva, and Miss Susie Brucks were located. It read:

Dear folks:
Just to let you know the sad news. The *Jeunesse* raided here last night. They destroyed everything in our house and killed Irene. They left me for dead too. If you are still there and can, please come over. I *need* you. My heart is near breaking—but God.

Funeral will be as soon as the coffin is made.

The MAF plane circled yesterday and dropped a note. We gave them proper signals that we wanted to be evacuated. They were to send a helicopter which I'm waiting for so anxiously.

God is faithful.

Love,
Ruth

I learned later that this note saved the lives of these missionaries by warning them of the imminent danger. They had not realized the urgent need of getting out to safety. An hour after the note reached them they were taken to Idiofa by some soldiers in an army truck, escaping just in the nick of time as the *Jeunesse* had already surrounded their station for an attack.

When I took the note out to Paka who was impatiently waiting for it, anxious to be on his way, Gaston met me at the door.

"Come on over to the dispensary and let me dress your wound," he said kindly. The wound was still bleeding and under ordinary circumstances needed stitching, but for lack of the proper facilities Gaston cleaned it thoroughly with disinfectant and taped it. I am sure God's healing hand touched it, for, though not dressed again until three days later in that hot country, it gave me no further trouble.

It must have been close to ten o'clock when I returned to the house. I am sure that our little four-room house was one of the nicest, most comfortable, and attractive little homes in the African bush. William Jantz, our missionary builder, had designed and built it of cement blocks in 1958 when I first came to Mangungu to teach in our central Bible school. Never in my previous twenty-six years on the mission field had I lived in a house providing so many conveniences. There was glass at the windows, hence no need of darkening the inside with closed shutters when it rained; I have always loved to watch the flash of lightning and the progress of a storm through the window. I still get a feeling of luxury just to roll shut a casement window. Instead of the customary outdoor facilities, there was an indoor bathroom with running water from two rain barrels under the eaves. (In dry season Lubambu kept the water running by fetching it from the spring, climbing up by a little ladder, and pouring it into the barrels.) There was even built-in closet space and an attic for storing supplies.

The furniture, made of hardwood by Congolese carpenters, was waxed and rubbed until it shone like glass. Among the most valued pieces of equipment, gifts from friends, was a Servel kerosene refrigerator, a Maytag washing machine run by a gasoline motor, a Perfection kerosene stove instead of the usual wood one, and a folding organ for enjoyment and relaxation.

The cream-colored walls, the crisp white Priscilla curtains at the living room windows, the waxed green cement floor, the colorful scatter rugs, all blended harmoniously for that homey atmosphere that every woman desires. Our little house always held out friendly arms of welcome whenever we came in from a village trip. We accepted it as a gift from the Lord and enjoyed it to the full.

And now everything was in shambles. Our once-beautiful haven of rest was now a place of carnage. Our suitcases with all our valuable papers, passports, and most treasured possessions were gone. Clothing, bedding, towels, typewriters, Irene's accordion, and everything else that could be carried off had disappeared. Many of the larger things had been hacked to pieces or demolished. Kerosene lamps lay shattered on the cement floor, the jars of mango sauce that Irene had canned the month before were broken, their contents spattered everywhere. The fire was still burning in the kerosene refrigerator but the glass on the freezing compartment had been smashed and the food swept out on the floor. (Later I saw the shell of the refrigerator, all its entrails removed, on the path leading to the village.)

All this time I was still barefooted and blood-smeared. I looked around in my room and in the corner of my clothes closet I saw a pair of white sandals. As I looked

farther, to my wonder and amazement I found every article of clothing I needed. Again how near and real the
Lord seemed. He upholds all things by the Word of His
power but He also counts the hairs of our head and knows
our every need. He had preserved my glasses and a pair of
shoes (things which the terrorists would never have left
had they seen them) and now with the dress Rebekah had
returned, I was completely outfitted. As I continued my
search I found a washcloth, a comb, a cake of soap, a tooth-
brush, and best of all a Bible, a gift from my father twenty
years before. And there was my *Daily Light* and a note-
book in which I had written some meditations. My every
need for escape had been supplied. No, I lacked one article:
a bag in which to carry these few personal necessities. Then
I remembered one made of native cloth, which I had discarded and consigned to the attic. Quickly I ran upstairs.
It was still there and big enough to hold all my treasures,
for treasures they were, straight from the hand of my
Father Who had foreseen and provided.

As I write these words, I am reminded of a poignant episode in the life of that Old Testament prophet Jeremiah,
who, at the bidding of Jehovah, had the unpleasant task of
condemning the sins of the Israelites. For his obedience
and unremitting activity he had been imprisoned in a dungeon and sank in the mire.

Ebed-melech, an Ethiopian eunuch, felt pity for him and
gained his request of the king to lift Jeremiah from the
abandoned cistern where he had been dropped to die. The
only way to free the prophet was to hoist him by strong
ropes, but ropes would chafe the skin raw. That thoughtful
eunuch took some "old cast clouts and old rotten rags and
let them down by cords into the dungeon." Then he called
to Jeremiah to put the worn rags and cast-off cloths under
his armpits under the cords by which he drew him up. A

strong and effectual deliverance was wrought by the ropes, but only a tender heart would think of the protection of the soft, emollient rags. I too had been delivered from death by the strong ropes of God's arm, and now He was supplying the "old cast clouts," the ordinary, commonplace, personal needs. What evidence of His loving care!

Though the utmost destruction and confusion prevailed in my house, I, standing there in the center of His love, somehow felt detached from and cared little about the material things.

> Let me hold lightly temporal things,
> I who am deathless, I who have wings!
> Let me hold fast, Lord, things of the skies,
> Quicken my vision—open my eyes.
>
> Show me Thy riches, glory and grace,
> Boundless as time, endless as space.
> Let me hold lightly things that are mine,
> Lord, Thou didst give me all that is Thine.
> —Unknown.

By this time the *Jeunesse*, joined now by the village people, had come back to plunder and carry off all that had been left from the attack. Hearing the noise of pounding and hacking from the direction of the other missionary residence, which had not been touched the night before, I looked to see them breaking down the door, then dragging things out. Here is where we kept the CPRA food supplies and other things such as soap, matches, salt, sugar, and cloth, which Irene had bought at wholesale to resell to the workmen at a much lower price than they had to pay at the *magasin* (store). Men, women, and children with boxes or pieces of furniture on their heads filed down the path to deposit their loot in the village and to return for more.

It made me sad when I recognized some of our own school children and older village friends entering into the plundering. But I could not condemn them too severely. They had little, and here was a chance to get something for nothing. Why should they not profit?

They were entering my house, too. I went into my bedroom and locked the door. The drapes on my windows were still drawn and again I was thankful for the privacy. I heard the clattering of dishes and silverware in the kitchen. Tables, cupboards, and heavier items of furniture were being pulled across the floor. Repeatedly they tried the door to my bedroom and pounded loudly demanding admittance. My heart beat fast, but I remained quiet. Then I heard them in the attic dragging drums down the stairs and tearing up the floor boards. Some were nailed down and had to be pried off. Several times I feared they would break through the plywood ceiling and come tumbling into my room.

A hand reached through the broken window in my room and started tugging at the drapes. I hid on the floor behind the bed. In a moment the drapes were gone, and one man was poised, ready to climb in through the window. I arose from my hiding place and said,

"What do you want? Just tell me and I will hand it to you." I gave him the chair he pointed to and some clothes hangers. I continued handing out books, chairs, and smashed objects through the window until only the larger items of furniture—bed, desk, dresser—were left. Mercifully these were not taken before I was moved to the dispensary. After that the greedy invaders took over.

It was late afternoon when Pastor Luka came to the window. He looked drawn and tired. He told me that the president of the *Jeunesse* gang who had made the attack was outside. He had come to Luka demanding a sum of money, threatening,

"If you do not give it to me, we will torture your Mademoiselle."

"*Pardon, pardon, pardon;* no, no, no," said Luka alarmed. "Don't torture her. I will get the money for you."

So Luka had been to the village seeking the ransom money from his friends and relatives. May the Lord bless those who contributed to save my life. *I* do not know who they were but He knows them by name and He has promised that even a cup of water given for His sake will be noticed and rewarded. He Himself will recompense them.

"Now," said Luka, "the president says he still needs a wrist watch."

Since I was lying on my left side, my watch had escaped their notice when I was left for dead and, of course, the leader knew that I still had it. I took off my prized Omega and handed it out the window to Luka.

In a little while Luka re-appeared with the president himself.

"He wants to give you *mbote* (greetings)," he said.

There he stood, a young man with a hard glint in his eye. He wore a loin cloth, a knife at his belt, and carried a bow and arrow. He had evident qualities of leadership, and I could look only with pity upon one so deluded and ensnared by communism. Here was the one who had led the attack in which Irene was killed. He too was one for whom Christ died. The thought flashed into my mind, Don't be afraid of those who can kill the body. After that there is nothing more they can do. Only for a moment he stood while we stared at one another then he said,

"*Bika mbote*" (Farewell) and he was gone.

Luka said, "I have found some men to dig the grave, but

no one will make the coffin. We will wrap Mademoiselle in a mat to bury her." Then he added, "We have decided that the best place for you to spend the night is in the dispensary. Come with me now."

I left my room and followed Luka as he led the way to the dispensary. We passed the garage where Irene was still laid out on the cot. There was no time to linger—just a quick final glance, and we hurried on. Clearly there was still danger even though the *Jeunesse* leader was gone.

Gaston was waiting at the dispensary. He had been busy all day taking medicines out of the well-stocked pharmacy, trying to hide them in trunks in the village, for there was fear the pharmacy, too, would be looted. As he checked the dressing on my wound, his wife Marie came in. He handed her a cardboard box of penicillin injections, and said,

"We are leaving for Kanga now."

It was a distance of at least forty miles on foot to their village. There were six children, the youngest a babe in arms, the second one a toddler who also would need to be carried, and the third youngest, from an injection wrongly placed, suffered a paralyzed leg, which he dragged pathetically. Doubtless Gaston hoped that the injections would serve as "pass letter" along the way if stopped by the *Jeunesse*, for every Congolese loves a *ntunga* (needle or injection). Once again we committed one another to the Lord and they were gone.

Nyanga, the carpenter, had repaired the broken shutter at the dispensary window. He came now with a bowl of rice and a side-dish of eggs.

"Eat, Mademoiselle," he said solicitously, "My wife prepared this for you."

How I appreciated their thoughtfulness! I had not eaten

all day and should have been hungry—but could coax down only a few bites.

It was getting dark when Luka returned.

"We have just finished burying Mademoiselle," he reported. "Just a few came to the burial. We prayed over her grave, but did not sing. The *Jeunesse* may be lurking around and we didn't want to attract them."

I could understand their concern, and I was grateful that Irene's "earthly tent house" had been laid to rest, awaiting that great Resurrection Day when:

". . . the Lord himself shall descend from heaven with a shout, with the voice of the archangel, and with the trump of God: and the dead in Christ shall rise first: Then we which are alive and remain shall be caught up together with them in the clouds, to meet the Lord in the air: and so shall we ever be with the Lord." I Thessalonians 4:16, 17.

We talked a little longer and then Luka said, "I am going now, Mademoiselle."

The thought of being left all alone in the dispensary terrified me. I pleaded,

"Please don't leave me here alone. Let me sleep in the village—anywhere. I will be perfectly quiet; I will sleep on the floor; only don't leave me here alone."

Luka was disturbed but seemed at a loss to know what to do. After a while he said, *"Bika mbote. Nzambi lunda nge"* (Farewell. May God take care of you).

He went out the door and I heard the click of the padlock. I listened to his footsteps become fainter and fainter, receding in the direction of the village. I was left alone with the haunting fear that the *Jeunesse* would return to loot the dispensary or perhaps set fire to the building, leaving me trapped inside.

Darkness fell. All was quiet.

6
A Night to Remember

*I will both lay me down in peace, and sleep;
for thou, Lord, only makest me dwell in
safety.*

Psalm 4:8

A sense of utter loneliness and desolation possessed me as I groped my way to the examination room and, climbing on the high table, I put my head on the straw pillow that Gaston had left for me. There was not one ray of light to penetrate the darkness, not one sound to break the eerie stillness. The door leading from the pharmacy to the examination room was locked. The terrorists would not know that all the valuable medicines had been removed. They would return in the night to finish their looting and I would be trapped inside and tortured, or so I reasoned in my misery. My soul was as dark as the night. Oh, why had God not taken me Home with Irene? How much better it would be to die than to live and fall into the sadistic hands of the assaulting rebels!

"Call upon me in the day of trouble: I will deliver thee, and thou shalt glorify me." Psalm 50:15. It was when David, the anointed king of Israel, was being pursued by his enemies that the Lord so instructed him. This word was for me now; I was in trouble; I would call upon the Lord and deliverance would surely come. When Peter began sinking beneath the waves and cried, "Lord, save me," *immediately* Jesus stretched forth His hand and caught him. So He did for me now. *Immediately* He was there saying, "Fear not."

Then God Himself again began to pour heavenly refreshing into my afflicted soul. Was there ever another who could comfort like unto Him? The removing of human companionship only made more manifest His divine companionship. *Near* was too distant a word to express the proximity of His presence—He was dwelling within—nearer than breathing and nearer than hands and feet. He bade me fear no more the fury of my persecutors because He was at hand to protect and deliver. He Who had framed the worlds by the Word of His mouth and had gone to so great expenditure to purchase me from eternal death would not now let me be overwhelmed nor perish before the malice of men. He reminded me that "the servant is not greater than his Lord, neither he that is sent greater than he that sent him." Jesus, my Lord, had been persecuted, despised, rejected, forsaken, and hated without a cause that He might become *my* Savior. He willingly "gave his back to the smiters and his cheeks to them that plucked out the hair" and "He hid not his face from shame and from spitting." Should I then, the least of His servants, be discouraged or despair because of my light afflictions?

Many years before when the Lord had first called me into His service, He had given me as my life verse Philippians 3:10,

"That I may know him, and the power of his resurrection, and the fellowship of his sufferings."

I had accepted and believed and appropriated these truths with my whole heart, but never before this climactic hour had I been so intimately cognizant of the depths of their meaning. My heart melted in adoration as I recognized the privilege that my Lord was granting me to know Him in the fellowship of His sufferings in a way I had not ever experienced or even thought possible before.

This unspeakably close and joyous fellowship was mine *now*, at this present time, but there was more—much more awaiting me in the future. Paul, the apostle, says,

"Whatever we may have to go through now is less than nothing compared with the magnificent future God has planned for us." Romans 8:18, Phillips Translation.

And impulsive Peter, who by painful experience knew whereof he spoke, tells us not to be unduly alarmed at the fiery ordeals which come to test our faith, but:

"You should be glad, because it means that you are called to share Christ's sufferings. One day, when He shows Himself in full splendor to men, you will be filled with the most tremendous joy." I Peter 4:12, 13, Phillips Translation.

Then He took away fear of death as with new freshness the Scriptures were opened to my now-hushed soul. I was reminded of the second chapter of Hebrews, which I had recently memorized. Had not Jesus, God's Son, taken a body of flesh and blood like unto ours that He might bear our sins? Through His death on the cross had He not also broken the devil's power of death? Why should I then be held in bondage to that *fear* of death, when He Who is all-powerful had already set me free? My triumphant, resurrected Lord had come forth from the grave in that same body to assure me that death is but the door to life—an abundant life in His Father's house. So why should I fear death when for me to vacate the body would take me into the very presence of the Lord, for to die is gain?

Suddenly, with a startling crash, the stillness was broken by loud claps of thunder. This was my Father's voice coming as a seal to my meditations. First, He had spoken intimately through the still, small voice within, assuring me of His tender love and care and now He was speaking in lightning flashes and thunder claps of majesty and power. Torrents of rain began to beat down upon the metal roof of the dispensary, a melodious message of encouragement to my listening ears. I knew that the *Jeunesse* would not be skulking about in the storm.

> Oh, could I tell, ye surely would believe it!
> Oh, could I only say what I have seen!
> How could I tell, or how can you receive it—
> How, till He bringeth you where I have been.
> —Unknown.

7
A Goodly Heritage

Thou hast given me the heritage of those
that fear thy name. Psalm 61:5
Yea, I have a goodly heritage.

Psalm 16:6

In reminiscence I could turn back the hands of time to another unforgettable night fifty-three years ago. I was a child of six. My parents, my younger brother, my four sisters, and I were fast asleep in the little three-room, tarpaper-covered shack. We were pioneers in the sagebrush-covered country of the Snake River Valley of southeastern Idaho. Our farm was near the Blackfoot Indian reservation and the sight of a swarthy Indian with his feathered headgear and long shiny black braids incited more respectful fear in my impressionable heart than even the call of the coyote or the sound of a rattler.

That day there had been a community jack-rabbit drive in which several thousands of these harmful rodents were killed. Stores and places of business were closed while bankers and merchants hilariously joined the farmers in the sport of driving the rabbits from their holes into a common corral where they were clubbed to death. The Indians, evidently incensed by this wholesale slaughter of their meat supply, threatened to take vengeance. I had overheard the adults discussing it.

"White man kill rabbit; we kill white man."

Lying alone on the couch in the kitchen, I was awakened out of a sound sleep with a start. The curtains rustled in the breeze, the moonlight threw eerie shadows on the wall. I was sure the Indians were prowling around outside and at any moment would come bursting into the room. And then they would scalp me! My heart pounded wildly; I could hardly breathe; I couldn't even scream for help. In my distress and helplessness I thought about the Lord Jesus, the Friend of little children. In our Bible picture scroll I had seen a beautiful picture of the Good Shepherd holding a little lamb. Suddenly I felt the presence of the Lord; I knew He was there and He was holding me in His strong arms. He would not let the Indians harm me. In a moment all fear completely vanished and I slipped into a peaceful slumber.

That Bible picture scroll loomed large in my childhood. It must have been a purchase extravagant for our parents in their struggling circumstances, but it was of inestimable value in the spiritual education of their offspring. Only on Sunday afternoon, and under adult supervision, were we permitted to look at those brightly colored pictures, taking turns to roll the scroll carefully as mother told us the stories. Wise parents they were to relieve the drabness of the prairie and the shack with good artistry depicting Bible stories. They were wise also to let us look at it only on Sundays, for that made it something extra special, leaving indelible marks on our minds. The picture and the story of the Good Shepherd Who went in search of the lost sheep and brought it back on His shoulders rejoicing was my favorite. I never tired of hearing it.

My parents had known each other as children in Germany. Both my grandfathers were overseers of large estates, hence were financially comfortable, having hired help in their homes and governesses for their children. Moreover, Grandfather Hege and Grandfather Horsch were elders in their respective Mennonite churches. These godly patriarchs ruled well their own households all week; on Sundays they stood in their pulpits holding forth the Word of God to instruct, encourage, warn, and edify their humble, hardworking parishioners.

When my father, Ulrich, was in his late teens, his parents brought their family of twelve children across the Atlantic to America, the land of opportunity. Several years later my mother, Elisabeth Horsch, accompanying an ailing sister, arrived in the Mennonite community of Paso Robles, California. My Aunt writes:

> Elisabeth and I embarked in Bremen. We were not listed as emigrants but rather as tourists, for we planned to go back home after two years.

But as friendship with the Hege family was renewed and as handsome Ulrich seemed to pay marked attention to her, Elisabeth abandoned the thought of returning to Germany, preferring adventure and a home with the one she had grown to love in America. They were married in the little adobe church, still a landmark in Paso Robles, on June 15, 1899. While teams of tired horses dozed lazily at their hitching posts outside, Grandfather Hege and another elder spoke earnest words of admonition and exhortation to the young couple. I have been told that the service lasted for two long hours!

Neither Mother nor Dad, reared in happy, comfortable homes, could have anticipated the struggle for existence that awaited the western settler. Among the treasured manuscripts in our family files there is a sheaf of letters in the old German script in my mother's clear handwriting. They tell a continuous but uncomplaining story of seven years of courageous toiling and praying together to make the barren California soil yield a living for a growing family. After repeated drought and crop failures, a move for the family seemed imperative.

Having heard that the United States government was offering land on inviting terms to settlers who would bring it under cultivation, a group of California farmers including my grandfather, my father, and my uncles made a survey trip to the Snake River Valley. Satisfied, they returned to prepare their families for a move to American Falls, Idaho. In September five families (ours including Hilda, the oldest, Esther, Lydia, and me the youngest of eighteen months), with all their possessions from kitchen utensils to livestock, boarded the train heading northeast. The passengers must have occupied a whole coach; the possessions a whole boxcar!

We lived in tents until the men could erect what were supposed to be temporary shelters for that first winter. That little black shack built by my father as a provisional dwelling for his family was to be our home for the next ten years. Though to the casual observer it held no attraction, to me it was the most blessed place in all the world.

One of my close friends tells me that I am more than ordinarily fond of home and family, that she can sense my inner reluctance to leave them, my almost uncontained joy in seeing them after an absence. I suppose I have always had this light affliction which no medication can cure. I remember poignantly the painful, pining, pathetic nostalgia of homesickness I experienced as a child when I had to leave that shack and spend some time as a companion to an older cousin who was homesteading at a distance of some two hours' ride by horse and buggy. With every turn of the wheels the ache in my heart became greater. It was something that had to be borne alone, for no one knew that at night, when the kerosene light was extinguished, hot silent tears of longing were dampening a little girl's pillow. No palatial mansion could even begin to compare with that humble little black shack and its dear occupants.

As I think of that Idaho home, other memories come rushing in so fast that they fairly trip over one another: the call of the lone coyote for his mate; the wind sweeping across the sagebrush prairie with snow or dust blowing through the cracks of our abode; summer's scorching sun beating down on the parched land, blistering our bare feet, or the severe cold of winter numbing our fingers and toes so that mother had to bring in a pan of snow and with it rub our limbs until they tingled; floating down the shallow irrigation ditch using mother's old, discarded washtub as a boat; playing house with my cousins who lived a mile down the road; or spending a night with them on the two occasions when the angels left a baby at our house. My only brother James was their first delivery and two years later, my sister Marie. Hanging on the wall above my bed was a picture of a most beautiful guardian angel carefully guiding two little children across a narrow bridge spanning a deep ravine. Such a lovely being could be trusted to bring a precious little baby safely down to earth from the celestial abode!

What adult does not remember his childhood Christmases, especially when a tradition of acts and deeds and decorations has been built up over the years? In our home Christmas began in November when mother started kneading the *Lebkuchen* dough. Soon after, our dolls disappeared and then some mornings we were mystified to find tiny scraps of gaily colored material on the kitchen floor. (What we did not know was that each doll was being decapitated to receive a brand-new Sears Roebuck head. Mother often sewed and knitted late into the night, making dainty and elaborate clothes for our dolls, while father sawed and planed and hammered to turn out beds to fit them.)

Shortly before December 25, our father gave us each 25 cents and we spent all day in town doing our Christmas shopping. Never since has one single quarter yielded so much elasticity to purchase gifts for every member of the family. Unquestionably there were patient shopkeepers in Aberdeen in those days!

Then there came the day when Dad announced that he was leaving early the next morning to cut down an evergreen tree. That meant that the great day was very, very close. Sentries were posted all day long, blowing on the frozen window panes to melt little peepholes to watch for my brave father's return from many miles away with the prized trophy. Just once our kind Dad, against his own better judgment, yielded to our pleadings and took Lydia and me along. Though Mother bundled us up in as many woolens as she could muster, the deep snow on the roads so retarded our progress that when we returned at night we were chilled to the bone. From then on the previous parental decision, that this trip was *not* for children, became final and unalterable.

When the morning of the 24th finally dawned we fairly tingled with excitement. After dinner on that day only mother and father were privileged to stay in the kitchen to prepare for the *Kristkindlein* (Christchild). We six were consigned to the bedroom. Once when the door opened I was near enough to get a glimpse into the kitchen.

"What did you see?" questioned my sisters eagerly.

"The *Kristkindlein*," I answered without hesitation. I was not intentionally telling an untruth. I thought I had seen a shining Presence, and who are the elders to say that I hadn't? Surely only the Christ Child could bring such heavenly joy to the hearts of little children, and I know too that my parents were not working alone. Jesus Himself was there in that humble kitchen to encourage and bless their efforts to make His birthday a happy time for their little flock.

Then came the blissful moment when the door was swung wide open and we were invited to pass through. I can still feel the thrill of it. There stood the tree, resplendent with dozens of wax candles glowing softly. We did not notice that the tinsel was tarnished and full of candle drippings. To us it was gloriously beautiful. And there under its branches were the dolls, each in its own little bed. But it was not yet time to touch them. First we must sing *"Ihr Kinderlein Kommet"* ("Come Ye Little Children") and *"Stille Nacht, Heilige Nacht"* ("Silent Night, Holy Night"). Next the sweet story from Luke 2 was read or recited from memory and my father led in a prayer of thanksgiving for God's unspeakable Gift. Not until then were the gifts given out, and we could handle them to our hearts' content—and eat cookies and apples, as many as we could hold. I do not recall when I awoke to the fact that the Christ Child did not actually come from heaven in person to bring the gifts on Christmas Eve, but when I did, it was not a shock or even a disappointment, for was not the One whom the shepherds worshiped in the manger still the Giver of every good and perfect gift?

As Christ's birthday was the highlight of the year, so Sunday was the highlight of the week. My parents were ever diligent to make it a day of reverence and happiness for children. The thought of missing church on Sunday morning never entered our minds unless, of course, we were snowed in. On such occasions we held church at home. It was a five-mile ride to the little country meeting-house. We drove in the old spring wagon (sadly in want of springs!) in the summer and in the low sled in winter. Since we had only one team of horses, the ride to church was taken very leisurely. My father insisted that these tired animals who had worked faithfully in the fields all week should not be driven hard on Sunday. They too were due a day of rest. On the way, then, we always had time to memorize the *Golden Text* of the lesson.

When we returned from church, mother took off her black silk wedding dress before dinner (it had had several alterations) and father hung up his matrimonial suit. On Monday morning mother would carefully brush these Sunday clothes, making any necessary repairs, to be ready for the next Lord's day. They became shinier and more threadbare with the passing of the years.

Usually on Sunday afternoon the whole family were in on some kind of activity. Sometimes Mother and Dad would turn the rope and we practiced our jumping; on pleasant days we took walks through the fields; in winter we made snow ice cream; on rainy or stormy Sundays we looked at the Bible picture scroll or listened to mother tell stories. She could hold us spellbound with her tales about her girlhood in Germany—as I grew older and a little more discerning I could detect a wistful tenderness. Then she would tell us about ourselves, things that happened when we were smaller, about our *baby* days. How we would chuckle! I would feel all warm inside when the story was about me. I suppose the others felt the same about themselves. Sundays were really "sunny" days for the large family in the little tarpaper-covered shack.

Daily at the breakfast table my father read the Scriptures to us in his native German; then he tore from the Scripture calendar on the wall the meditation for the day, reading that also to his brood; finally he prayed, never ceasing to thank God for His goodness to him and his family.

The Apostle Paul wrote to young Timothy, reminding him that from early childhood he had been familiar with the Holy Scriptures, which open the mind to salvation through believing in Christ Jesus. I too had been familiar with the Holy Scriptures from early childhood. I have no recollection of walking down the church aisle to indicate my conversion, for this was not practiced by those stolid and sterling Mennonites, but I do know that as a child my mind was open to the salvation which comes through believing in Christ Jesus. I also know that the Lord Jesus was real to me.

The happiness of our family as we children so freely accepted it was seldom if ever marred by spoken worries on the part of my parents nor were there even undertones of personal problems. It is well that we understood very little of the heavy burdens gradually more and more weighing upon my father's strong shoulders and Mother's more fragile ones. We were so loved and so welcome in that little shack that their every thought was for our welfare.

This personal experience, written in excellent German by my mother entirely unknown to us, appeared just after her death in a German religious magazine, *Christlicher Bundesboten*, April 1947. Its translation follows:

Behold the Fowls of the Air . . .

Many years ago, far out in the west, there stood a small hut such as the pioneers built to shelter their families. Full of courage and zeal for the work before them, the young couple with four children ranging from two to six years of age, moved in. There were many hardships to endure, but they were young and made adjustments easily.

At the beginning it was necessary to drive a distance of eighteen miles (with horse and wagon) to get the mail. All necessary food supplies, and the doctor, in case of emergency, had to be fetched from there as well.

The winters were bitterly cold; it was a struggle to keep family and cattle from freezing. The grain, which was scarce and expensive had to be hauled a long distance, and had to be well protected and kept for the needs of the live stock.

Summers were very hot, but one soon got used to

this. Dust storms blew over the freshly plowed land, but here too one accepted the unavoidable, and rejoiced in being able to get on with the field work. The immediate surroundings of the little hut underwent a change that first spring. Bright flowers blossomed in the garden, which also yielded an abundance of vegetables and potatoes. How good everything tasted!

With much hard labor the first few years passed, but the expected results were not forthcoming. One trusted in God and encouraged oneself in Him for strength to carry on the struggle for existence. Meanwhile the family had increased by two. The four oldest children went to school, and the two little ones played merrily outdoors. All were happy and carefree as is the way of children.

But things did not go as was hoped. The small capital was used up; then sickness came into the family and misfortune to the livestock. Doctor and hospital bills had to be paid and medicine was expensive. Horses and cows were needed to keep the little farm in operation. It was hard to know what to do and anxious worry crept in as an unbidden guest.

One lovely summer day the farmer went into the field to cut alfalfa. The hay had a good stand that year. Also the other land under cultivation gave promise of a good harvest, so, at least, there would be plenty of food for the livestock. But where should food and clothing be found for a family of eight? Burdened and heavy-hearted he sat on his mowing machine. He urged the horses on as a deep sigh for help ascended to his heavenly Father Who had promised not to forsake His own. Suddenly, just in front of the wheel, he saw a nest of tiny, helpless birds. It was too late to stop the horses and in another moment the heavy wheel of the mower would crush the poor little creatures. And then something unexpected happened. A rock which lay concealed in the way lifted the wheel over the nest so that it remained unharmed. The little birdies opened wide their mouths to receive the worm which they instinctively expected from their mother. And now our friend brought the horses to a halt and went back to see what had happened to save the lives of the little birds. As he contemplated the wonder, many comforting thoughts came to his mind. Could not the Father in heaven who had protected the birds, also keep him and his family? Once again trust and confidence were restored and he went on his way rejoicing. And help did come, not as he had expected, but in God's way. His thoughts are not man's thoughts, but His ways are always best.

Frequently in the coming years the family was in need and in straitened circumstances, but always help came. "Those who trust in the Lord shall not be ashamed." At the end of the way all who put their trust in Him will acknowledge, "He hath done all things well."

> Commit thy way, oh weeper—
>   the cares that fret thy soul,
> To thy Almighty Keeper
>   who makes the world to roll;
> Unto the Lord who guideth
>   the wind, the cloud and sea
> Oh! doubt not, He provideth
>   a footpath, too, for thee.

(Translated from the German hymn *"Befiel Du Deine Wege."*)

For ten years the courageous, relentless struggle continued and then, at the repeated invitation of my uncle John Horsch, the farm was sold and the family moved to Scottdale, Pennsylvania. At first it was all very exciting—new clothes for everyone, the farewell activities, the five-day train ride, and the anticipation of meeting new relatives.

Uncle John and Aunt Christine and my city cousins heartily welcomed us into their home. We children especially were all new to one another and found much mutually to admire at that first flush of acquaintance. But eastern city ways and western country ways did not easily mix, and many were the verbal clashes—not physical clashes, because both the Horsches and the Heges were being reared as "defenseless Mennonites"—over which were the better. I can't recall that either side ever admitted defeat.

We attended school in Scottdale. Here again it was difficult to adjust to new ways and new schoolmates. Though my parents were by now naturalized citizens of the United States, we continued to speak German in the home and amongst our friends and relatives. We were considered, for that reason, as being pro-German. These were the years of World War I and a wave of German hatred engulfed the country. Many were the taunts that came our way because of our heritage, but we were encouraged by the precepts and example of our parents to hold our peace and accept them quietly. Then came the signing of the Armistice of November 11, 1918—an unforgettable day, especially for those who had loved ones on the front lines. Though I was only thirteen, I shared the deep sense of relief with my parents whose affections were inextricably attached to both sides.

The following year Lydia and I were sent to the farming community of Kidron, Ohio, to attend the Mennonite catechism class preparatory to baptism. We each earned our board by helping in a home where there were children. With the ending of the war unemployment increased and my father lost his job. Later my parents and the two youngest came to Kidron, where Dad was soon busy on the farm again.

In February of 1920, when I was just fifteen, the family moved once again, this time to Wellington, Ohio, where Dad worked on a stock farm. Since there were no Mennonites in town, my father visited every congregation in the community, and after due deliberation, consultation, and prayer, the Baptist was chosen as our Church home. The denomination was not the criterion upon which my parents based their decision, but rather the touchstone now was the emphasis on the fundamentals of the faith as revealed in the Word of God. Later I became a member of the First Baptist Church of Wellington, Ohio, which subsequently had a vital influence in the molding and direction of my life.

With hard work and encouragement from home I was able to attend college. By scrupulous saving, my earnings during the vacation months paid for most of my tuition and I did housework for my board and room. When I got my degree from Wheaton College in Illinois, my mind was made up as to my future—I would be a teacher of mathematics. Those were depression years and many experienced school teachers were out of work, so I gratefully accepted the offer of a fifth- and sixth-grade room in Chatfield, Ohio, with the promise of a high school position the following year. However, this was not to materialize, for five months later, in February of 1931, during a message by Miss Alma

Doering, veteran missionary of the Unevangelized Tribes Mission of Congo, I gave myself to the Lord for missionary service in that land.

I remember the struggle that went on in my heart that morning as I thought of giving up all my well-laid plans of a profession and a home and family of my own. Although I do not remember what the speaker said, the Lord showed me that my body was the temple of the Holy Spirit, and I was no longer my own, for I had been bought with the price of the precious blood of Jesus Christ. No longer could I withhold from Him the purchase for which He had paid so dearly, and that morning by a personal transaction I deliberately yielded to Him first place in my life and became His by right of self-surrender. He answered with an inward peace and joy not known before. Nothing but the Lord's unmistakable call could ever have made me leave my home and family, who never had seemed more dear and precious to me. Not until then did I know that it had been my mother's prayer that God would call at least one of her six children to the mission field. I stood in awe and wonder that the Lord had ever chosen me, the least likely, in answer to that prayer.

I continued to teach until the end of the school year, doing everything possible to prepare for the new goal. All were feeling keenly the weight of the depression, and we were told that as an initial amount it would take thirteen hundred dollars to send a missionary to the Congo field. Where was this staggering amount to be found at such a time? Surely my parents, much as they longed to, could not provide it. Among my treasured possessions destroyed by the terrorists was a letter in my father's handwriting, dated February 1931, in which he expresses regret at being unable to help me financially and encourages me to trust more fully in the Lord Who had never failed us in the past and would surely prove Himself all-sufficient in the future.

I praise God for my little home church. Without exception they took up the challenge and gave unstintingly of their time and labor and means, often at a real sacrifice. The ladies of the Missionary Society met in all-day sessions to sew and to pack boxes, which the men of the church made according to specified instructions. I am sure that never was more loving labor and forethought expended on the equipment of any missionary.

Much credit is due to H. K. Finley, my pastor at that time. He stood firmly in the van as he led the church into a new appreciation of missions and their responsibility in carrying out the Great Commission of preaching the Gospel to every creature. During those months scores of letters went out from his desk—some soliciting the prayers and interest of the surrounding churches and friends, others to the Unevangelized Tribes Mission Board for detailed information, and others to various shipping companies.

On June 28, 1931, at a service solemnized and blessed by the Lord's presence, I was formally set apart for mission work abroad by the laying on of hands of pastor and deacons. Sunday, October 4, was the day set for the reaching of the financial goal of thirteen hundred dollars. When the service began we were still short of the objective, but the offering that morning sent us flying over the top. All stood and with full hearts sang the Doxology. *"Praise God from Whom All Blessings Flow."* With our God there was no depression. He still owned the cattle on a thousand hills and stood ready to turn them into tangible cash for His trusting children.

It was on a cold, wintry evening, January 25, 1932, that the members of the church gathered in a body at the railroad station for a final farewell. As I boarded the train someone quickly pinned a corsage on my coat—a last token of love. God had spoken to the little Baptist Church in Wellington; they had heard and now they were sending me forth. How loyally they had all worked, what generous helpers they had proved to be, and how greatly the bonds of love had been strengthened during those months of preparation! I stood on the back platform, waving my handkerchief until the train rounded the bend and they were out of sight. The lump in my throat was getting bigger, threatening to choke me, until suddenly the tears that had been welling up all day flowed unrestrainedly and splashed in big drops on the friendly carnation.

In New York I joined Miss Maude Hogeland, who was going to the Congo under the same mission. A few days later as the *S.S. Westernland* pulled slowly out into the Atlantic I stood on the deck, waving farewell to friends and my brother, who represented the family. It was bitterly cold. They stood in a huddle on the pier singing,

"Go ye into all the world and preach the Gospel, and lo, I am with you always." Their voices carried across the widening space until they died away in the distance and the last home ties were broken.

Since that first sailing and the present eventful night in the dispensary, exactly thirty-two years had elapsed. Eighteen of those years (1937-1955) were spent serving under Baptist Mid-Missions in Venezuela, South America. Now, as I reviewed God's leading in my life, I too could say,

"I will sing unto the Lord, for he hath dealt bountifully with me." Psalm 13:6. He had brought me through dangers from rivers and floods, from wild animals and infuriated men, from illness and accidents, and with a strong hand He had delivered me out of them all. As the rain continued to beat its recitative on the dispensary roof, I relaxed into a blessed sleep.

8
A Day to Remember

For I, saith the Lord, will be unto her a wall of fire round about, and will be the glory in the midst of her.

Zechariah 2:5

I awakened at the first streak of dawn, refreshed in body and with a deep calm within at the remembrance of my tryst with the Lord during the night. Would the helicopter come for me today? Would there be another encounter with the *Jeunesse?* Should I perhaps try to get to the airport in Idiofa, twenty-five miles away? Or should I wait on the station until help came? These were some of the questions that occupied my mind as I held up my Bible to catch the rays of light coming in through the air vents under the roof. I opened it to Psalm 46 and began reading, "God is our refuge and strength, a very present Help in trouble. Therefore will we not fear. . . ." I continued to the fifth verse: "God is in the midst of her; *she shall not be moved:* God will help her, and that right early."

This was my answer. I would not leave the station but would await God's help right here. I read on—

"Be still, and know that I am God: I will be exalted among the heathen, I will be exalted in the earth."

This was a message directly from the Lord to my inquiring heart, confirming the decision made. I need not dread what lay before me for God was in the midst and whatever might happen, He would be exalted among the heathen.

There was a knock at the window shutter.

"Mademoiselle, are you all right?" It was Akiem's voice. I opened the shutter and presented myself at the window to substantiate the fact that I was unharmed.

"I walked around the dispensary several times last night. Everything was quiet. Thanks be to God that you are safe," he said.

Then Davidi, the teacher, came up and handed me two

bananas and a bottle of hot tea through the window. Later
he brought a washbasin and warm water in a pail for my
morning toilette. How concerned they were for my well-
being! I prayed for protection and provision and safety
for them as well as for myself.

By that time Luka had returned with the key and un-
locked the door. His wife, Marcelene, accompanied him
with a basket from which she pulled a skirt and blouse and
handing them to me said,

"If you need these, Mademoiselle, you can have them."
I recognized the articles of clothing as some she had obtained from me for a few pennies several years before. This
was a sacrifice, I knew, and I appreciated her thoughtfulness. I thanked her as I returned them to her, assuring her
that the dress I had was adequate for my needs.

More of the women came in to greet me.

"*Matondo kwa Nzambi*" (Thanks be to God), they said
fervently and with evident relief when they saw how well
I had survived the night. But none of them tarried very
long. Pastor Luka came in for consultation.

"We want to help you escape," he said. "The car is still
undamaged; the *Jeunesse* have not found it. We know a
chauffeur in Luembe and he can take you to Idiofa to the
airport."

How thankful I was for the clear direction I had received that I should not try to leave the compound—"She
shall not be moved." When I told Luka about it he was
satisfied.

"We will wait," he said, "Perhaps today the *avion* will
come for you."

(We did not know then that already the bridges on the
alternate route Irene had taken on Thursday had been destroyed so we would never have reached Idiofa.) We then
agreed that I should stay in the dispensary with the door

and window shutters closed so that any enemies sneaking around would not suspect that I was inside. Once again I was left alone behind a securely closed door, but this time I was very conscious not only of the reality of the Lord's presence, but also that outside many friendly eyes were on the dispensary watching to see what would happen and ready to come to my assistance should the need arise.

I had no watch, but it must have been about ten o'clock when Laurant, a Bible school student, opened the door.

"Luka sent me to get you," he said. "The village people are coming to plunder. We have put down a mat for you on the floor of the new hospital hut. Someone will be staying with you there."

He stepped out of the door to check again, and seeing no enemies around he said,

"All is safe. Follow me." Quickly he led the way over to the grass hut; I stepped inside and without another word he closed the door and left.

In a little while Nyanga entered and sat down on the floor.

"I am going to stay with you, Mademoiselle," he said. "Don't be afraid. I have a big club just outside the door. No one can come to harm you."

Doubtless ninety-nine per cent of his brave talk was to bolster up his own waning courage. The day before I had sent for him to make Irene's coffin and he had not appeared. Now, without being asked, he volunteered some weak excuse about being too busy and not being able to get away. But I understood his fear and talked to him of Irene's present state—at Home with the Lord—and assured him that her body being wrapped in a bamboo mat for burial was of no vital concern.

We sat silently for a while; then like a shot, without warning, he leaped up and darted out the door. Grabbing his club, he sped down the path toward the water, shouting back over his shoulder,

"They are coming. Follow me." I tried to run but my legs were weak and my feet dragged. The next instant his flying figure was out of sight.

"Nyanga, Nyanga, Nyanga," I called weakly, but no answer. Behind me I heard the sound of running feet about to overtake me. I took a few more steps into the tall grass beside the path and quickly dropped from sight. My pursuer was coming menacingly nearer and nearer. In a moment he would be upon me. As if whispered into my ear, I heard,

"*God is our refuge and strength . . . God is in the midst of her. . . . Be still, and know that I am God.*" The footsteps halted; I could hear his breathing and I could sense his baneful presence before I could see him.

I looked up into the sin-darkened face of a man with a most awful evil countenance. Towering over me, he was dressed only in a loin cloth and carried a bow and arrow.

"I'm going to kill you," he glared threateningly. "See this?" He pointed to a little pouch tied to the end of his bowstring. "This is what we put on the arrows to kill you."

Again the whisper—*God is my refuge . . . I will not fear.* Calmly I said,

"You can kill me, but you can also show mercy. God in heaven is watching you and He wants to have mercy on you. He loves you and sent His Son Jesus to save you. If you kill me I will join my friend in Heaven, but if *you* die where will *you* go?"

Immediately the malevolent expression on his face melted before my eyes. His hands fell to his side. For a moment he stood apparently in deep thought. Then with a decisive voice he said,

"No! I will not kill you, but I will hide you. You have many enemies. Come, follow me. I will take you to a safe hiding place."

I did not trust him but there was nothing else I could do. I got up and followed as he led the way deeper into the tall grass. After going quite a distance we came to a low scrub tree. He said,

"You stay here and hide. I will go and tell Luka where you are." I crouched low in the shade of the tree where he left me. I wondered if he were going to seek out the rest of his gang to tell them where he had hidden me. I did not believe he would hunt Luka, but all I could do now was wait and pray.

How much time elapsed, I do not know—perhaps a half hour—before I heard someone approaching rather stealthily through the grass. I crouched lower, if that were possible, and waited breathlessly. Then a familiar voice called my name, and the next moment, to my great relief, I was looking into the face of a friend. Kakoy and his wife Katembo had seen the episode. Waiting until the coast was cleared of all rebels, they had sent Kitoko, their young son, to get me. They put me into another hospital hut. Katembo brought me some water to drink, a bowl of rice, and some greens. Then she went out saying, as she closed the door,

"I won't be far away. If you need me just call. I'll be nearby watching the door."

What a consolation it was to know that I was still the object of concern to our people! I was not utterly abandoned. Their love for me made them willing in some measure to suppress their own fears and do what they could.

It must have been about two in the afternoon when I heard a commotion outside. Katembo pushed open the door and said excitedly,

"Come quickly. The *avion* is coming to get you."

I rushed out and saw a little Piper Cub circling low over-head. My heart missed a beat—at long last they were coming to rescue me! A Gospel of John tied with a long string of bandage was thrust into my hand.

"They dropped this from the plane—read it." With bated breath I tore off the bandage and found the note tucked inside, written in the Kituba language. It read,

"If Mademoiselle is dead, lie on the ground; if she has gone to Idiofa, wave your hands above your head." There was a postscript in English: "If you are safe, wait. We will come with a helicopter to get you."

I waved my arms desperately, pleadingly. The little plane circled once more even lower and then mounting it veered off across the valley.

As I stood there leafing through the Gospel of John a second note fluttered to the ground. It said,

"If it is safe to land, sit on the ground."

But they were already gone! Oh, why hadn't I seen this before? The enemy would have had me despair of help. As I re-entered the grass hut and Katembo closed the door, I was torn between hope and doubt—hope, because they had seen me alive and would surely send a helicopter immediately to rescue me. And doubt, because I had not given them the signal to land. I found out later when talking to Chester ("Scotty") Scott, the pilot of the plane, that the last note was not meant for me. It had been left in the Gospel by mistake. The clearing in front of the dispensary was not large enough for any plane to make a landing.

I waited in solitude only a short time, then the door was pushed open and the stocky figure of Zechariah, pastor of the Luembe Church, entered guardedly.

"It's me, Mademoiselle; I have come to sit with you."

He stepped across the high sill and closed the door. He was carrying a bow and arrow, the same sturdy type and size as those carried by the *Jeunesse*. Leaning his weapons against the wall, he sat down on the edge of the bamboo bed. His face showing resolution and determination, faithful, wholesome, unassuming Zechariah's presence inspired fresh courage and strength. Like Jonathan, Saul's son, who went to David in the wood where he was hiding from his enemies, and strengthened his hand in God, so Zechariah had come to strengthen *my* hands. It was *my* turn to breathe a fervent

"*Matondo kwa Nzambi.*"

For some time we sat in silence, each occupied with his own thoughts. Then suddenly the silence was broken by loud angry voices. Zechariah sprang to his feet, grasped firmly his bow and arrow, and peeked through the bamboo slats of the door.

"They have come," he whispered. "Just remain quiet where you are."

Outside the agitated argument increased in intensity. I knew they were looking for me. Again the quieting words *. . . I will be exalted among the heathen. . . . Be still, and know that I am God.* He alone could control this excited mob and cause even the wrath of man to praise Him. They were coming nearer and nearer. Then with an angry vigorous push the bamboo door flew open and I was face to face with my pursuers. They had discovered me.

Zechariah stepped into the doorway with bow and arrow in hand.

"You can't enter here," he said with firmness.

One (the leader of the gang, I learned later) stood glaring at me across Zechariah's shoulder. He lifted his bow and, fitting the arrow to the string, aimed it at me. Unflinchingly I looked straight into his eyes; slowly he lowered his weapon. Others crowded around and wanted to push in but Zechariah held his ground. He sat down on the high sill of the narrow doorway, his bulky figure filling the space. Then I noticed that outside there were other faithful Congolese attempting to hold back the mob. Zabulon and Samuel, the two teachers from Leumbe Nene, also armed with bows and arrows, were moving among the crowd arguing, persuading, pleading, cajoling, in an effort to calm the irate mob.

This new gang was evidently from Luembe Nene village and our teachers, knowing they were bent on murder, had followed them. It seems that the coming of the plane had aroused them to action. They thought that I had called the plane by the use of a telephone which I had hidden somewhere about my person. Doubtless they feared that I would call the soldiers to take vengeance on Irene's death by strafing the villages. Another ordered me to take off my glasses and placed an arrow preparing to let it fly. At that moment the leader intervened and made him put it down.

"Leave your glasses on," he commanded.

I was glad to obey. Then he pushed his way past Zechariah who, seeing the leader's anger abated, gave way and let him pass. Instructing his men to stay outside, this terrorist president sat down on the edge of the bamboo bed and began to converse.

"Where is your telephone, Mademoiselle?" he questioned. I assured him that I had no telephone.

"Then how did you call the plane that flew over a little while ago?" I told him that I had no way of calling help except through prayer. This gave me an opportunity to talk to him about an all-powerful, prayer-hearing and prayer-answering God whose love to mankind was expressed by sending His only Son to die on the cross for the sins of the world.

"And He loves you and wants to save you too," I concluded.

He listened, then said thoughtfully,

"I wanted to kill you all day yesterday but God didn't want me to." Showing me his arrow he said,

"See that dried blood on here. That is the blood of the three priests we killed. I wanted your blood to be on here too, but God didn't let me do it." He added, "It is good that the *avion* did not come to get you because we would have killed you all."

This information startled me as I was still expecting the helicopter momentarily. I began to understand *why* I had been kept waiting so long and *why* I had not seen the note (which I supposed had been meant for me) about giving the signal for a safe landing. I questioned him,

"Should the plane come now to get me you would let me go unharmed, wouldn't you?" I realized that it was better for me to be left and to die alone than for others to lose their lives in an attempt to rescue me. He was wise enough to know that a man will give anything in exchange for his life and shrewd enough to see his opportunity to drive an advantageous bargain for himself.

He said craftily, "If you give me the keys to your car I will tell my men to let you go."

I told him that I no longer had the keys to my car, so they were not mine to give away.

"But you can get them," he responded cunningly.

Zechariah produced a scrap of paper from his pocket on which I wrote a note to Luka explaining the situation and asking him to come with the car keys.

After what seemed a long, long wait the messenger returned *without* Luka.

"He says he can't come now." He had given no reason for his refusal and I felt uneasy. Did he not realize that this was a matter of life and death? But the terrorist leader was undaunted.

"Come, we will go and find him," he volunteered as he arose.

I looked at Zechariah who nodded encouragement.

"I will go with you."

By now it was late afternoon, almost sundown, and we formed an unusual procession moving down toward the village of Mangungu. I was walking beside Zechariah with the *Jeunesse* president in the lead, and his gang trailing behind us. The procession grew in numbers as the curious village folks fell in line at the tail end—far enough away to be able to run should danger threaten, but near enough to see and hear what was going on.

We found Luka in the house of his uncle, a big-built, fearless African (not a Christian) who was one of the village leaders. I was ushered into the house and offered a chair while the rest went outside to confer about the car keys. It was dark when Luka came in to report that after much dickering the gang leader had gone off content without the car keys but with a thousand francs in his pocket. Doubtless the chieftain unwittingly acted on the proverb, "A bird in the hand is worth two in the bush." With roads torn up and bridges out he must have seen the advantage of taking the tangible cash in preference to the car; besides, not being the chief leader who had led the attack on the mission station, he might have foreseen difficulties in claiming ownership to the vehicle. I do not know where or how Luka obtained the money for the settlement made, but he, too, seemed satisfied.

"The church will need that *camion* to take evangelization trips in the future," he explained. Though I had serious misgivings that the car would be spared for such a mission, nevertheless I rejoiced that once again the Lord had delivered us from the hand of the enemy.

After some discussion it was decided that I should spend

the night in the home of Luka's uncle. All cooperated to make me as comfortable as possible. From somewhere my own camp cot reappeared and was set up in the corner of the room. For my evening meal, Luka went through the village and collected some of the loot the villagers had taken from my kitchen the day before. There was a can of chicken-rice soup, some mango jam, some powdered milk, part of a loaf of bread, some cheese, and a few other familiar foods. Luka's aunt brought me a pail of cool water for bathing. I was learning something of the blessedness of possessing *nothing*, and yet possessing *all* things.

Another day had passed. The longed-for helicopter had not come, but the Lord Himself had been a Refuge and a wall of fire round about so that no harm had come to me. All my needs had been supplied and no *good* thing had He withheld from me. I was thankful to be among friends and, stretching out on my cot bed, I was soon sleeping the sleep of utter exhaustion.

9
Pearl of Great Price

. . . When he had found one pearl of great price, [he] went and sold all that he had, and bought it.

Matthew 13:46

There are those well-meaning souls who, upon hearing of Irene's martyrdom, of my harrowing and distressing plight, and the harassment and abuse of missionaries on other stations, would seriously question the wisdom of sending us in the first place. They would decry the fact that such promising young people bury their talents and sacrifice their lives to the work of taking the Gospel to pagan lands.

"What a waste," they say, "that a consecrated young woman should thus throw her life away. Irene Ferrel was completely wrong in her thinking. The Africans did not ask her to come to them nor did they need her. They are happy in their own pagan beliefs and superstitions. Why thrust Christianity, a western religion, upon them?" And so they reason.

We ask then, were we missionaries all deluded by some highly altruistic bent? Was Irene wrong in laying down her life that these people might hear and know of Christ, the one true and living way to God? Is the price too great to pay? It has been rightly said that the blood of the martyrs is the seed of the church. Were *they* too wrong?

I firmly believe that Irene's blood, soaked up by the hot, parched Congo soil on January 25, 1964—that once strong, vibrant body buried in a shallow grave—will, as the grain of wheat that falls into the ground and dies, bring forth *much* fruit and yield an abundant harvest of souls for God's own glory. When the Merchant found the goodly pearl, costly though it was, He gave ALL He had to redeem it. Was it worth ALL we had to take the message of God's redeeming love to pagan Africans? The record of the lives of those to whom we went has spoken and will yet speak for itself.

I was awakened before dawn by the noise of many running feet. My host came through his bedroom door, picked up his bow and arrow from where it was standing in the corner of the "guest" room, and blew out the light that had been burning low in the lantern all night, thus leaving the room in total darkness. Cautiously he opened the door a crack to look out. I strained my eyes and ears to see and hear. What could be the trouble now? Were the *Jeunesse* taking up their pursuit again so early in the morning? I knew that two *Jeunesse* presidents had already been paid off, but there were other roving gangs who might be seeking a share in the spoils. We had no guarantee that the same ones would not be back to exact more ransom money. The running continued. My warrior-host had by now slipped out into the darkness, closing the door behind him. I knew that he had befriended me and for this I was most thankful, but whether he had left the house to follow friends or fight foes was a question that troubled me. I heard some low secretive talking outside and then all became quiet. Praying for safety for my friends and sanity for my foes, I waited.

When at dawn Marcelene (Luka's wife) came in to greet me I questioned her about the cause of the commotion. She told me that chief Nzadi was calling the village men together, instructing them to arm themselves and guard the mission grounds so that any *avion* coming for me could make a safe landing. Aware of the threats of the *Jeunesse* to stage a massacre should an attempt be made to rescue me, they stood ready to fight. Was it worth our ALL? Again I praised the Lord for loyal friends in this time of need, but I prayed that there would be no bloodshed on my account.

Nzadi was the head chief of our large Mangungu village. He wore the little patch of monkey fur in his hair and a tier of tightly fitting copper bracelets on each arm as emblems of delegated authority. For many weeks he had come regularly to our early morning Bible studies in the Gospel of John. It was an encouragement to look into his upturned face as he listened with rapt attention, drinking in the Word. Faith comes by what is heard, so we were not surprised when Nzadi lingered after class one morning. I invited him into the living room where we could talk undisturbed. The lesson that morning had been from John 6 where Jesus said,

"I am the bread of life. . . . If any man eat of this bread, he shall live for ever." After once more explaining the way of salvation to him, he prayed,

"God, I am a sinner, but I want to leave my life of sin and follow You. I believe Jesus died for my sin and I now eat Him and take everlasting life." By this simple act of faith Nzadi passed from eternal death unto eternal Life and at that moment this heathen chief joined the family of the redeemed and thereby became my brother in the faith. In this relationship he was now seeking to defend and protect me from the enemy, and my heart warmed at this manifestation of his concern.

When Luka came in we discussed the situation. I feared that in case a helicopter should come to rescue me, the pilot, seeing the station surrounded by armed men, would be discouraged from making a landing. He might believe the warriors to be enemies, in which event his aircraft could easily become the target of terrorist arrows.

After consultation with Chief Nzadi, Luka returned to report that the village men had been alerted to defend any rescue operations; however, they would not now be surrounding the station. Then he said,

"We are going to hide you in an empty house near the dispensary today so that you will be near at hand when the *avion* comes for you." He led the way by a back path through the grass to an unoccupied hut, which was being used as a storehouse by one of the Christian families. It was located near the road leading to Luembe village but near enough to the dispensary so that there would be no delay in reaching the clearing should the anticipated airlift come that day.

A table and chair and a bamboo bed had been moved in for my comfort. Katembo sent me some boiled eggs and rice and coffee for breakfast. In solitude, but with a thankful heart, I was partaking of these provisions when the door was pushed open cautiously and Zechariah entered.

"I have come to stay with you today until the *avion* comes," he announced simply as he laid his bow and arrow on the table and sat down.

Kadiandundu Zechariah was the pastor of our newest local church in the village of Luembe-Nene. For many years he had been recognized as a spiritual leader in that village and when the group of Christians there was organized into an independent local church, Zechariah was unanimously chosen to be their pastor. To me he was the pastor with the shining face: humble, unpretentious, no formal education whereof to boast, but with a special portion of the love of God shed abroad in his heart—a love that overflowed to all around him regardless of color or social standing. From village to village he trudged on foot, preaching to his own people the good tidings of salvation by faith in Christ. He returned from these trips with glowing, inspiring reports of conversions and glad acceptance of his message.

Irene and I helped him to get a bicycle, which was a most appreciated and prized possession. When the soldiers came in and began plundering in the villages, Zechariah brought his *velo* to the mission for safekeeping. He had been a real pastor to his flock—seeking the backsliders and lifting up those who had fallen by the way; comforting the sorrowing and giving a helping hand to lighten heavy burdens; strengthening the weak hands and confirming the feeble knees; feeding the Christians from the Word of God and by precept and practice encouraging them to become personal soulwinners. It always gave me a lift to fellowship with Zechariah, for he himself was hungry for new truths from God's Word. Now, his very presence brought cheer as he sat there dozing in the chair. Was Zechariah worth our ALL?

Watching faithful Zechariah reminded me that Kusa Luka, the pastor of the Mangungu local church, was another one of God's choice servants. For many years he had served the mission as *kapita* or boss of the working crew. Though he was faithful in the task assigned to him, in his heart he was not satisfied, for he wanted to serve the Lord as a pastor. But how was he to prepare for such work when he had neither means nor opportunity to go to Bible school? Then, to his great delight, Bible school was opened in Mangungu right at the outskirts of his very own village. Luka was one of the first applicants. He worked hard during the three years of training and when the missionaries were evacuated at the time of Congo's independence, he was named pastor of the church and left in charge of the station.

We returned after one year to find Luka weighed down with pastoral problems. During our absence many had been baptized and admitted into church membership who were not born-again Christians and who gave no indication of being new creatures in Christ Jesus. Consequently there was dissatisfaction and bitterness and quarreling among the members. The old chapel on the station was about to fall down; the roof was leaking like a sieve so that services had to be dismissed when it rained. The material building was like a thermometer of the spiritual temperature of the church and it indicated grave illness and need of revival. Prayerfully and persistently, in private conversation and in public Bible classes, we taught what Christ had to say in His Word about the Church, which is His body, of which He Himself is the Head, whose members are indwelt and quickened and united by the Holy Spirit. Slowly we saw these truths take hold of Luka, and with rejoicing we witnessed the accomplishing of work that could never have been done by white missionaries.

One day we were happily surprised to see a group of the brethren, commandeered by Luka, pulling down the old building. Within a few days work was begun on a new one. The believers did all the planning, contributing the labor, and meeting expenses from their own tithes and offerings. Our part (Irene's and mine) was to encourage and admire and pray as the new structure went up. It was made of Congo building materials: poles, bamboo, grass, and pillars built of sun-dried brick. The backless benches were of hand-sawed boards from the forest, nailed on both ends to short thick logs buried in the dust floor. I am sure that no imposing cement block structure put up by missionaries could have united the church to work together as harmoniously nor would it have given half the satisfaction and pleasure experienced by them in looking upon their own completed handiwork.

The spiritual as well as the material building had been renovated. A new membership list was made, which included only those who were faithful in their attendance at Sunday afternoon Bible study and Wednesday afternoon prayer meeting. Luka's messages were marked by a new ring of conviction and we sat under his ministry with profit. He was fearless and uncompromising in his denunciation of sin and prompt to apply church discipline on the authority of the Bible. I had noticed that during the last months he had seemed under special compulsion to warn his people repeatedly of the predicted apostasy in the last days. He warmed to the preaching of the second coming of Christ, especially the rapture when the Lord Jesus Himself would descend from heaven to take His Church to the place of many mansions where they would be forever with Him, inevitably concluding with the admonition of I John 3:3, "Everyone who has at heart a hope like this keeps himself pure for he knows how pure Christ is." Was Luka worth our ALL?

It was a blessing to see the companionship that grew up between Pastor Zechariah and Pastor Luka. They consulted on all major decisions of church discipline and practice and cooperated in the building programs. Luka, being the older and more experienced, was the recognized leader. Their aim, as ours, was the establishing of a local New Testament church in each of the surrounding villages. I thought of the baptismal services last month. The candidates had been thoroughly examined and questioned by the deacons and elders of both churches. My heart thrilled to the clear-cut testimonies of some of the women—these who had been long kept under were coming into their own through the power of the Gospel. The two men and two women from Mudjimbila, some distance away, were baptized in a creek near their own village as a testimony to their own families and friends. After coming up from the water we gathered in the village schoolroom to partake of the Lord's Supper, remembering Him in His death and coming again—the first time in that village. Afterward Samuel, the deacon from Luembe-Nene, rose to his feet and said solemnly,

"Brothers, now that there are some baptized believers in this village, we pastors and deacons from our two organized churches must come every week to teach them and to seek others to add to their number until they too can have their own local church here in Mudjimbila."

Ntshundu Benoit, who was assistant teacher in Bible school, with his wife, Pauline, and two foster children, had already fled to his own village. He was from our Balaka station of the Bawongo tribe. Benoit, as the owner of a village *magasin* (store), had been financially successful and was sought after as salesman by the Portuguese merchants. But no lucrative offer could turn him aside from his purpose of full-time Christian service. He came to us after completing his fourth year of study at the Kafumba Bible Institute, a Mennonite Brethren school. His zeal for the Lord was both refreshing and contagious. With his family he lived in one of our student dormitories. Besides the classroom activities, he supervised the daily work hours of the students and kept a fatherly eye on them day and night. He knew his own people and could handle them far better than we could. We had prayed for a white missionary couple and were disappointed when none was forthcoming, but again we were made to recognize God's superior wisdom in giving us Benoit just at that time.

Luka, Zechariah and Benoit—there was something about that trio, watching them consult, plan, work, and pray together, that always brought fresh courage to the sometimes wavering spirits of the two single women laboring alone on Mangungu station. Even now as I was hidden in the storeroom, the remembrance of them brought renewed strength and confidence to believe that God's work would go on in spite of Satan's wrathful attacks. It was worth our ALL!

Then there were the primary school teachers: Kindua Zabulon, Nzuela Samuel, Kaziama Elaston, Mandundu Teofile, and others who had served loyally. Nkiedi Richard, the primary school director, came to see me, greatly concerned about the future of the school children.

"What shall we do? They have burned the schoolhouse and all our books. How are the children going to be taught now?"

He knew that in his position of leadership his own life was in danger.

During the course of the day, again and again, the door was pushed open warily to admit one or more of the faithful church members. With deep emotion in their voices betokening a grieved heart, they said,

"We haven't eaten; our hearts are full of much sadness for you; we want you to get out to safety."

Or

"We are praying constantly for you. We want the plane to come for you. God will not leave you here to get killed."

Teresa Ntschunsh, one of the old Christian women, came and lingered a long time. She spoke only the tribal language so our exchange of conversation was limited, but there she sat with tragedy in her eyes, her whole being bespeaking sympathy and concern. We were experiencing vividly the truth of our oneness in Christ, regardless of race or color.

"As the human body, which has many parts, is a unity, and those parts, despite their multiplicity, comprise together one single body, so it is with Christ. . . . So it happens that if one member suffers all the other members suffer with it. . . . Now you are together in the Body of Christ, and individually you are members of Him." I Corinthians 12:12, 26, 27, Phillips Translation.

This is the "pearl of great price" for which the Lord Jesus Christ gave all that He had—His very life's blood—to buy it and make it His own special treasure. True, the

terrorists had destroyed all that I had of material possessions, but that which was most precious could not be
touched by them. That which mattered most still remained.
No Communist-inspired attack on our mission station could
in any wise alter His purpose for the Church for it was
built upon the Rock, Christ Jesus, and the power of death
and hell could not prevail against it. Though I could not
begin to guess what trials, hardships, and sufferings might
yet await those Christians, I knew that His Church could
not be destroyed. This trial by fire would but serve to
purify His own.

> When through fiery trials thy pathway shall lie,
> My grace, all-sufficient, shall be thy supply;
> The flame shall not hurt thee; I only design
> Thy dross to consume, and thy gold to refine.*
> —George Keith.

* "How Firm a Foundation," in *Inspiring Hymns* (Wheaton,
Ill.: Singspiration, 1951).

10

A Stronghold in Trouble

The Lord is good, a stronghold in the day of trouble; and he knoweth them that trust in him.

Nahum 1:7

I am sure that each one of the missionaries caught in the Communist net during those days of terror in the Kwilu province of Congo could tell a thrilling story of miraculous deliverance. Our God has no favorites! His mercies are upon all and His eyes "flash back and forth over the whole earth to display His strength on behalf of those whose heart is full of integrity toward him." II Chronicles 16:9, Berkeley Version. While I was a captive of the *Jeunesse* at Mangungu, fellow missionaries on other stations were also passing through days of anguish.

There were the missionaries at Kandala to the southwest of us, held as semicaptives of the *Jeunesse* for forty-eight hours. They saw their station, which was thirty years in the building, reduced to smoking ruins in the space of one fiery night. James Bertsche testifies,

"During the hours of greatest confusion, tension, and danger, there was a quiet reality of God's presence which was a new experience for us all. While all about us was uproar, fire, and menace, ours was an inner calm of spirit which we shall never forget. Verses which we had known by memory for years and taken more or less casually for granted, now suddenly became dramatically relevant and precious."

At Mukedi to the southeast of us were those missionaries who answered the emergency call from the Catholic mission at Kilembe where the three priests had been massacred. They, at the risk of their lives, went to rescue six nuns and a Belgian teacher. With the help of the chief of Mukedi village and his sons, all lives were spared and airlifted from the mission airstrip by the MAF planes. At the close of that most trying day when all were safe, Peter Bullar writes,

144 · *We Two Alone*

"Through this day, too, God has been faithful. He specializes in emergencies."

At the Iwungu Station to the northwest of us there were nine adults and eight children to whom MAF had dropped a note similar to ours. I did not know about this earlier note-drop to them, but have since learned that as the pilot circled for their answer, all the missionaries stood with hands at their sides to indicate they would stay. They knew there was fighting in the Iwungu area. Both soldiers and rebels had come to the mission for medical help. Several soldiers had been killed and Mulele's men had discovered that the medicine supposed to make the bullets turn to water was ineffective.

After the skirmish Miss Wyla Weekley, the missionary nurse at Iwungu, was called upon to suture some serious bullet wounds for the terrorists—a face, a hand, a chest, all torn apart. Still the missionaries there did not feel that they were in any grave danger themselves, so they resolved to stay with their people to continue the primary and secondary schools and medical work as usual.

It was not until Sunday, January 26, that they realized the seriousness of the situation. The missionary plane flew over Iwungu again and dropped this crayoned message:

> Prepare immediately to evacuate. Situation grim. Helicopter coming. Don't delay. Don't question.
>
> Kandala burned. Missionaries in danger. Helicopter will return. Roads dangerous—get out by helicopter. Everyone must get out. Men also.

An added note written hastily with pen revealed bewilderment and indecision. It said,

IRENE IS DEAD. ~~GET~~ Stay on station. Wait for helicopter. GOD BLESS YOU.

Darrell.

The writer of the penned note was Darrell Champlin, the anxious father of three of those eight children at Iwungu. He and Louise had made a trip to Kikwit for medical care and, when the trouble broke suddenly without warning, they were caught in that city fifty miles from their children.

It was through this note Winnie learned of the death of Irene, her dear sister and companion. Stunned by the news, the missionaries made preparation for immediate evacuation. It was Thursday, four days later, that three fighter planes swooped low over the villages near Iwungu to frighten and drive off the rebels. The next moment a scout plane zoomed at treetop level over the station. It was followed immediately by three UN helicopters. The nine missionaries, a Belgian priest who had taken refuge with them, and eight children climbed aboard as the U.S. Ambassador's plane circled overhead. Even before the doors could be closed they were airborne and on their way to Kikwit and safety. Miraculously they had been delivered from the rebels surrounding Iwungu.

Of this event Clarissa Barton wrote,

> We waited until Thursday morning for the helicopters to come. At all times, someone was in listening range of the short-wave radio—tuned to the AMBM [American Mennonite Brethren Mission] frequency. The various reports of destruction, of friends in need, and of the rescue of others brought sadness, concern, and rejoicing in turn. . . .

In those days of waiting, there was busyness in preparing meals for the whole group (we continued to eat and sleep in our house). There was fear at night as in the dark every normal sound had an interpretation of possible danger. In the daytime, the tension was eased by the carefree running, laughing, and playing of the missionary children. And through it all there were the promises of the Lord, steadfast and sure.

The rescue was so sudden and accomplished with such speed that the fifteen-year-old daughter of a Congolese pastor of a distant village was missed in the operation. Elisabeth, a secondary student, had been frightened by the noisy roar of the numerous planes and had hidden. In the excitement she was left behind. Miss Barton brought this to the attention of the UN commander when they landed at Kikwit. He felt they should go back—the Congolese girl was as important as an American. Miss Barton accompanied the soldiers back to rescue Elisabeth, who had by this time come under the care of one of the faithful Christians at Iwungu. As the helicopter was once more airborne, this time with Elisabeth aboard, Miss Barton wrote,

> As we took off I waved good-bye to Jacques and I wondered what would be the outcome of all this. How would he and the other Christians fare?

Later Elisabeth returned to the Kwango via commercial airline. Thus the rescue of the Iwungu Station was completed.

During the December holidays we had visited our Swiss colleagues, the Rev. and Mrs. August Eicher, at Balaka, some seventy miles north of us. They were concerned then about our safety in the trouble area and had given us an urgent invitation to their station, where all seemed quiet with no foreboding storm clouds on the horizon. It was a comforting thought to me that at least the Eichers were safe. They had experienced all the hardships and heart-aches and dangers of pioneer missionaries when they first entered the fierce cannibalistic Bawongo tribe in 1929. Now after thirty-five years of hard labor these faithful veterans were entitled to a respite.

Mr. Eicher, the legal representative of Baptist Mid-Missions, was a licensed medical worker. He was well known to the Congolese as *Munganga* (doctor). Balaka now had a large medical work carried on by an efficient staff of Congolese male nurses, with some 250 consultations daily. An increased number of village women were coming to the mission for delivery and *Munganga* was happy for the new maternity building, which was nearing completion. Balaka mission was as the hub of the wheel from which radiated some forty preaching posts manned by forty-six teacher-evangelists who taught over eight hundred children in primary school.

I was unaware of the tireless activity of MAF in dropping warning notes and checking on so many missionaries, therefore I had not known they had flown north to check on the Eichers also on Friday. Wes Eisemann, the pilot, reported:

> Approaching Balaka we noticed smoke rising on the horizon. We became anxious, thinking it might be the mission in flames. It was the commercial and government center of Kipuku being burned and sacked. All the government homes and offices were in flames as well as the stores. Trucks were being loaded with loot, and people from the nearby villages were carrying things away on their heads. When we circled over the

town, many of the people ran from fright or from pricking consciences. When we noticed some white-helmeted men pointing rifles at us we flew away toward the east, then circled back to Balaka. Before we reached the station we spotted the Eichers' truck on the road. We flew low over them. They stopped, got out and waved to us. We did not drop them a message because we were unable to think of any advice to give them. They had to flee since the government center about ten miles away was in flames, and that is what they were doing. We left them in the hands of the Lord, and proceeded on to Kintshua.

I learned later that the Eichers, unable to make their escape by truck because of impassable roads and destroyed bridges, had returned to Balaka. They had with them Miss Bremond, a Swiss friend from Hebron Station, and on the road back they picked up Mr. Angelo, a Portuguese merchant who was also fleeing. That same evening a truckload of bandits drove into the mission compound. They forced their way into the building and with repeated threats on the lives of the missionaries, they began looting the house and loading the plunder on their truck. Speaking of those tense moments, Mrs. Eicher writes,

> One of the group stood striking idly at the piano keys. I asked if he would like me to play a piece for them, and without waiting for an affirmative reply, I sat down and played the hymn *All to Jesus I Surrender*. With Miss Bremond we sang two verses, guns at the back of our heads all the time. Nevertheless, this was a real strengthening to us, and again we felt God's peace and presence.

The *Jeunesse* gang asked for Mr. Eicher's truck. Their Portuguese merchant friend offered his. It was nearly midnight when the *Jeunesse* in their truck and the two white men in the Eicher truck left for Mr. Angelo's place. Upon arrival they found that his place had already been looted and the truck was gone. So the *Jeunesse* seized Mr. Eicher's vehicle and drove off, leaving the two men to return to Balaka on foot.

A second gang came to loot the station on Saturday morning, but after an hour they left without doing violence to the missionaries. It was on Sunday morning that a third gang of terrorists armed with clubs, machettes, hammers, and guns attacked. This time they smashed the windows, dragged the missionaries out of the house, and abused them. They took their glasses, watches, Mrs. Eicher's wedding ring, and Miss Bremond's hearing aid, which they thought was a telephone. They ripped off Mr. Eicher's shirt and made him kneel before them. One of them proudly claimed to be the executioner who had butchered the three priests at Kilembe. He said menacingly as he brandished a huge sledge hammer and a long knife above Mr. Eicher's head,

"Do you know how we do it? We cut off the arms and legs and head and leave only the body to be put into the ground."

They ripped off his shoes and clothing and hit him on the head with the hammer; they dragged him through the dispensary while they looted the valuable medicines, which had been destined for the healing of their own Congolese people. Some of the older men from Balaka village were watching the abuse from a distance. They boldly approached to intercede for his life.

"We do not want to see his blood on our ground. Let him die in his own land. He came here many years ago to help us. He has helped us very much. Do not kill him. Let him go," they pleaded.

This seemed to soften the executioner. The captives were led back to the house where glasses and passports were returned to them. Then their assailants left.

However, it was only a short time before they heard a truck approaching. Knowing that they would again be the objects of insults and abuse, the three missionaries ran for the forest. Their friend, Mr. Angelo, ran in a different direction. They later heard of his harrowing experiences in making his escape through the jungles and swimming across two crocodile-infested rivers to Port Francquis, some one hundred twenty-five miles away.

For a whole week the missionaries hid in the forest, all the while being hunted by the *Jeunesse* who were bent on killing. Loyal Christians cared for them and brought them food. Mrs. Eicher writes of those days:

> Sentries stood guard. Always two stayed with us to see if it was necessary to move us to another place. During this time of hiding II Kings 6:18 was a blessing to us. Elisha's prayer became our prayer—"Lord, smite this people with blindness . . ." and He did! The *Jeunesse* never found us though they searched the forest for us.

The little MAF plane continued the search for the missing trio. The missionaries hiding in the forest heard the engines and saw the plane, but had no way of making their whereabouts known. The pilot, Gordon Fairley, tells of this search on Saturday, February 1:

> We pressed on to the village of the Congolese pastor some miles to the east. Solid jungle passed below us.

We circled the village; the people seemed terrified and ran to hide in the banana thicket. The village was yet unburned, a fate which awaited those who did not go along with the program of the terrorists. The note we dropped read . . . "If Eicher is dead, lie on the ground. If he is alive, walk in the general direction he went." The note looked lonely lying there on the ground untouched. We found no response.

We flew on south to Eicher's mission station at Balaka. There I found his brand new, and as yet unused, airstrip with about thirty deep trenches dug across it. The station was unburned but had obviously been sacked and looted. School books and papers were scattered all over the lawn. The place looked as lively as a cemetery. Next we searched all the villages and outposts in the area. No sign of Eicher and his two companions. . . . We looked everywhere imaginable including a couple of places Eicher liked to frequent. We were heavyhearted as we returned to Kikwit.

The account of the following day's search, February 2, continues:

Our first message drop was in the village of Munga to the south of Balaka. The message was the same as previously mentioned. The villagers immediately got a white cloth and headed down the valley northward toward Balaka. We circled several times to make sure. Irv Friesen searched the valley and entire area with Colonel Meyer's binoculars for possible clues. Next we dropped a similar note at Balaka village. The people pointed north. We searched the village and area north . . . no sign. We circled and dropped a note at Tundu

Mapepe, a possible spot of refuge, but no sign of life here. We searched the roads and noticed the ferry had moved since yesterday. We found no clue in this general area so flew over the Loango River for Port Francquis. Upon landing there the local Catholic mother superior informed us that there were no white folks in town except herself and two priests. We felt utterly baffled, didn't know what to do next.

Meanwhile there were new developments for the hunted trio. They were advised by their faithful Conoglese friends that the Bawongo *Jeunesse* were taking over the Balaka area, and that this gang was disposed to help the missionaries escape. Early Monday morning with a letter of authorization from the *Jeunesse* leader, and accompanied by their friends, the three started on the long strenuous walk to Balaka. Just before they reached the village they were turned over to members of the Balaka *Jeunesse*, who led them through the tall grass to avoid being spotted by unsympathetic gangs. Three chairs were brought out and they rested under the shade of a grove of trees. Many of the villagers came from hiding to greet them and to express sorrow at their plight. And then they heard the welcome sound of the MAF plane.

We will let pilot Gordon Fairley tell the story of that finding in his own words.

> Monday, February 3. After a word of prayer at the end of Kikwit runway we took off. On board with me this time were Angus Brower and Mr. Chaponiere. The latter had prepared an armful of notes in the native language to be dropped in the villages around Balaka. I gave Idiofa a wide berth due to the fighting

there. Soon we were in the search area. Right away we dropped three notes—one at a village south of Balaka, one at Balaka village, and one in a village north of there. Next we circled back to the first village. The people gave indication that the Eichers were alive and somewhere north of there. We then flew over Balaka village adjacent to the mission station. Mr. Chaponiere let out a yell, "There they are!" Sure enough, there was a long pole with a white flag on it and in the middle of the village center opening stood Mr. and Mrs. Eicher and Miss Bremond! After the long fruitless searching and discouragements, here they were— alive! To be frank we all felt a little choked up.

I made a circle back and made a very low pass right by the missionaries to check visually on their condition. As I came upon them I tossed out a note telling them to expect the arrival of rescue helicopters. Also a package of sandwiches fell their way to encourage them a bit. . . . The news was flashed all over the missionary radio network. There were shouts of praise all over the Congo.

The note tossed to the Eichers told them that they could expect the helicopter the following day. But quickly the MAF plane winged back to its base of operations. Colonel Meyer had his rescue crew ready. He ordered all four UN choppers to be refueled and then a hasty takeoff was made for Balaka.

Meanwhile at Balaka village there was great rejoicing that the missionaries were found and would soon be rescued. However, the low-flying plane had brought on another truckload of incited *Jeunesse* who came to investigate

154 · *We Two Alone*

and gave the Eichers a hard time. Finally they agreed to put sentries around them for protection until the planes came for the rescue.

Mrs. Eicher continues the story:

> Later we were permitted to sit out under a small grove of palm trees where many old men and women with tears in their eyes came to shake hands with us, and thanking God for us, committed us to His care.
>
> Then Mr. Eicher asked for a razor to shave off his more than a week's growth of whiskers. He had hardly finished when someone shouted *ndeke*. A plane was nearing the village. We started to run toward the clearing and saw that it was a big UN fighter plane. Then we heard shouts, *Bandeke yankaka!* (More birds).
>
> As we looked up toward the sky we were able to discern: one, two, three, and then four, helicopters followed by two planes. In perfect order they circled over us, and then one started to come down. The excitement was so great for us that our legs almost gave way the last moment. The helicopter came lower and lower and landed. We stumbled toward the open door where the UN officer stretched out his free hand to pull us in. In the other hand he held a machine gun, ready for any eventuality. The Congolese friends helped push us in glad that we were at last able to escape. May the Lord bless them and protect them as they exposed their lives to save us.

The next moment the Eichers and Miss Bremond were airborne, enroute for Kikwit. . . . The Lord is good, a stronghold in trouble. . . .

Time and space fail me to tell of all those who through faith proved the truth of the promises of God and were marvelously delivered. I would add just one further word of tribute to the MAF (Missionary Aviation Fellowship, Fullerton, California) who played an important and effective part in the rescue of the missionaries. Reporting on the Kwilu evacuation, the April issue of MAF magazine says,

"When MAF entered the Congo three years ago, one reason was: the potential need of emergency evacuation of missionaries. Now potentiality had become reality."

The two MAF planes, piloted by Wes Eisemann and Gordon Fairley, flew courageously into the threatened areas. When there was an airstrip "MAF wings suddenly became a bridge to life." Meanwhile June Eisemann stood by the radio in Leopoldville from 6:30 a.m. to 10:00 p.m. following every move on the Missavia transceiver, thus paving the way for the execution of the well-coordinated airlifts which followed.

Because engines were nearly due for overhaul, the UN Command advised that their services would be limited to actual rescues. This left MAF to do all the searching for the missing and fleeing missionaries through rebel-held territory, then to direct UN copters to the right spots for rescue.

Gordon Fairley writes,

> In all the intense flying over rebel territory, four flying outfits operated. Those were the UN, Air Brousse, Congo Air Force, and MAF. Of these only MAF came through without a single bullet hole. We feel this is significant and an answer to prayer for safety. Wes Eisemann and I both saw terrorists shoot at us, but miss. In the dozens of hours that our planes criss-

crossed that troubled area, not one shot found its mark. We fly on, continually grateful for His protection and this opportunity of service.

MAF was instrumental in evacuating well over one hundred missionaries and their children from the troubled Kwilu province. With them, we ascribe all the praise to the One Who directed their movements by working through them, supplying strength and wisdom for each day's operation.

11
Land of Intense Darkness

*The people that walked in darkness have
seen a great light; upon those who lived in
the land of intense darkness light has shined.*
Isaiah 9:2, Berkeley Version

Over a century ago Protestant missionaries forged their way into the jungles of central Africa, the land of intense darkness, with the light of the Gospel of Jesus Christ. Throughout the Congo are scattered the graves of devoted soldiers of the Cross who laid down their lives in faithful service. Besides the visible graves, there have been scores of dedicated missionaries who, like David Livingstone, left their *hearts* buried in this their adopted land, though their weary and toil-worn bodies have been laid to rest elsewhere by loving hands. No tombstones mark their burial places here, but their testimony lives on in the Christians whose lives were illumined by the eternal light of their torches.

A network of mission stations, which have stood as beacons whose rays pierced the surrounding darkness of heathenism, criss-cross the Congo. I would hazard a guess that there is scarcely a village in all of Congo that has not been touched by the light of the Gospel of God's Son.

The question is then raised: If the Gospel of Light has been so widely proclaimed in Congo over the past decades at the tremendous cost of the lives of so many of God's choice servants, why this widespread and vicious outburst of lawlessness by the *Jeunesse* now?

Light rejected only increases the intense darkness of the human heart, causing it to turn completely from righteousness to rage against God.

"This is the judgment—that light has entered the world and men have preferred darkness to light because their deeds are evil. Anybody who does wrong hates the light and keeps away from it, for fear his deeds may be exposed." John 3:19, 20, Phillips Translation.

So in the Congo multitudes have turned from light to walk on in darkness. As a result, Satan, the ruler of the darkness of this world, has taken over their minds so that they have put their trust in an utter fraud and are believing a lie. With the ancient poet we would re-echo the question: Why do the heathen rage? Why have the rulers of earth joined forces against God to cast His "shackles" from them?

Communism, a Satanic tool, shouts, "Let us stamp out the Light by destroying the mission stations and killing the Christians."

God's quiet antidote to the raging heathen is the bright and unfailing Light serenely shining on in the face of darkness powerless to swallow it up.

Communism defiantly snarls, "There is no God! Man is nothing but matter. We will cut and slash and destroy until we have freed man from his bondage to a God who does not exist!"

To this God calmly but unalterably affirms, "I am God; and there is none else. I will set my Son upon his throne . . . and he shall reign until all his enemies be made his footstool. He is King of kings and Lord of lords!"

The attack on our mission did not come altogether as a bolt out of the blue for as early as 1960, at the time of Congo's independence, in a secret manifesto of the leftist party led by Patrice Lumumba there appeared this revealing declaration:

> The greatest enemy of our initiative is the clergy; it has the greatest monopoly over the people. It is necessary to employ Russia to paralyze it. Never respect it and search to give it the greatest misery possible that it shall not have the means to oppose us to our enemies. Look for every false way to oppose it before the peo-

The author with Irene Ferrel.

The Bible School building at Mangungu.

Timothy's uncle, Timothy, and Rebekah with Irene and Ruth in front of the mission house.

The author with her African namesake.

The children in Irene's class holding the dolls she made for them.

Susie Brucks conducts a baby clinic.

Manuel, the evangelist, and his family.

Nurse Gaston giving the Gospel to the sick at the mission compound.

Patients waiting for treatment. The author hid in the hospital huts in the background.

Nelson, a Bible School graduate.

The road to a baptismal service at the river.

Children of Bible School students.

Irene and Minte with her antelope.

Congolese boys at their house.

Prepare immediately. To evacuate. Situation grim. Helicopter coming. Don't delay. Don't question! Kandala burned. Missionaries in danger. Helicopter will return. Roads dangerous. Get out by helicopter. Everyone must get out. Min also. Irene is dead. Stay on station. Wait for helicopter. Love, DARRELL

A replica of the bandage message dropped. The piece of torn sheet was about two yards long and four inches wide with an 18-inch tear at the end.

Evacuation by helicopter from Iwungu.

ple, even to its faithful, in order to change its doctrine and impose our doctrine which you know. Rouse the masses that they will never practice or believe the Christian religion in order that they may revolt more easily against all missionaries and priests. . . . The strongest weapon which can be used is the lie, for once masses are excited, the accused will see himself attacked and will not be able to compete.

The assault on Mangungu Station bore evidence to the fact that the leftists had succeeded in carrying out their aims, with the difference that the control had shifted from Russia to China, for now Peking and not Moscow was calling the signals.

In the *Peking Review* of March 20, 1964, Wang Lin, a reporter, praises the triumphant revolutionary development in Congo and eulogizes the dead "liberator" Lumumba. He writes:

Today, the Congolese people, inspired by their fallen national hero, have carried their national-liberation movement to a new stage.

In late January a patriotic armed struggle broke out in the Kwilu region, 300 miles east of Leopoldville, capital of the Congo. The declared aim is: Liberate our country from the imperialists, the neo-colonialists and their hangers-on. . . .

According to recent reports the area controlled by the armed Congolese people has extended from 110 to 5,800 square miles. The vast countryside in the eastern and southern part of the Kwilu region is completely under their control. The ranks of the armed patriots are swelling, having increased from only dozens at the beginning of the struggle to about 10,000.

Wang Lin's article continues as in bitter terms he denounces U.S. imperialism and the UN forces, which he labels "a U.S. tool for aggression." He concludes with this statement,

"No matter what efforts are made by U.S. imperialism in its attempts to hang on in the Congo, the people's armed forces will continue to fight on until they have won the final victory."

In an article of July 5, 1964, Robert Hewett, Far East correspondent for *Minneapolis Tribune*, says:

The wave of Communist-led tribal revolts in Congo is officially praised by the Red Chinese regime as "an excellent revolutionary situation." Peking has reasons to be satisfied. Red China is calling the signals through Peking-trained Congolese Communist guerilla leaders and unquestionably is smuggling arms to tribesmen opposed to the Leopoldville government.

This "glorious revolution," secretly planned and executed by these masters of deceit, was fast enslaving the unsuspecting masses, dragging them into the intense darkness of Communist dictatorship. My heart aches for our beloved Congolese. If they had but opened their hearts to the light of the Gospel, how different their fate would be!

James E. Bertsche, missionary of the Congo Inland Mission since 1948, has written a pamphlet published by C.I.M., Elkhart, Indiana, entitled, *The Profile of a Communist Offensive*. The pamphlet deals with the January 1964 happenings in Kwilu Province and gives "a heartbreaking account of people resorting to violence in the hope of achieving answers to unresolved problems." Mr. Bertsche, a student of anthropology and himself in the hands of the *Jeunesse* for forty-eight hours, is well qualified to give an analysis of the movement. He says,

"A massive, spontaneous, popular movement such as the *Jeunesse* rebellion must have some deep underlying causes." He then proceeds to enumerate the factors relevant to the situation. Succinctly, not only had there been a keen disillusionment after three years of independence, which brought none of the promised prestige and status to the common people, but on the contrary the national economy had steadily deteriorated. This, with prices of merchandise constantly soaring, had left empty pockets and empty stomachs, the basic ingredients of a highly explosive situation.

In the pre-independence years, Belgians were accused of discrimination. Independence did not end the problem. Contrary to Congolese expectations, discrimination continued as knotty a problem as ever with one slight difference. Following independence it was the Congolese who discriminated against the Congolese. The group of middle-class, trained, salaried Congolese who stepped into positions of leadership made it clear that they considered themselves superior to their rural brethren and were therefore entitled to special privileges, which they fully intended to maintain.

In the new government, federal funds had a way of disappearing. Roads went from bad to worse. Teachers went without pay. Many rural dispensaries were closed. Broken-down ferries and bridges remained unrepaired. Justice gave way to bribery. And certain supplies became available only to those in the inner circle of influence. For some time feelings of disgust, hatred, resentment, and revolt toward the new national government smoldered in the hearts of the common people.

Taking advantage of these conditions, an aggressive leftist political party was at work flooding the area with pro-East propaganda, while Radio Moscow was pouring in its

venom of hatred and malice against "U.S. imperialism."
Mr. Bertsche comments:

> It cannot correctly be said that the *Jeunesse* move-
> ment is a Communistic movement. Not one person in
> ten who participates has any idea of what Communism
> is or means. The mass does not support the rebellion
> because of any appeal of Communistic philosophy or
> dialectic. They participate because of personal reasons.
> But it may certainly be correctly said that the move-
> ment is master-minded and directed by Communists.
> We have in Congo now a classic example of Commu-
> nist maneuver and opportunism. Capitalizing upon an
> explosive situation of frustration and unrest, they have
> once again managed to provide clever leadership which
> is trained to trigger the penned-up dynamic of social
> tension and to channel it in violent directions that best
> serve their own ends. The movement serves as a
> "bandwagon" for anyone who has an axe to grind. . . .
> In brief, the dynamic of the movement lies in the
> massive discontent and frustration of a people.

The *Jeunesse* of Kwilu Province were led by Mulele
Pierre, who, according to the January 24, 1964, issue of
Time, went first to Egypt and then to Red China, where
he studied guerrilla tactics. He returned to Congo to his
own tribal area near Idiofa to set up secret forest training
camps for youth, to instruct them in methods of attack
and subversion. Their aim was complete destruction of all
government posts, commercial interests, and mission stations.

The roving, elusive youth is organized into *equipes* or
teams who sleep in forest hideouts by day, and gather
after dark at some prearranged place to get their assign-

ments for guerrilla action for the night. Each band has a president in command of the troops to direct their assaults, a secretary responsible for records and official letters, and a quartermaster in charge of the distribution of food for the group. Mr. Bertsche writes:

> The teams of a given area are under the authority of what is known as a *commandant de battalion.* In large operations involving an assault upon a center this individual is recognized as the superior officer of the individual team presidents. . . . As to overall direction the name of Mulele Pierre was constantly heard. He obviously was the accepted leader and guiding spirit.
>
> A striking feature of the movement is the choice of terms used among them. Rarely do they call each other by any other term than *camarade.* In accosting a stranger, invariably there comes this question: "Are you a 'partisan'?" He who affirms that he is, usually has to answer further questions as to the band to which he belongs, the name of the president, etc. If he is not a partisan, there follows a thorough inspection and grilling including among other things the emptying of his pockets and even spending a period of time on his knees under the disquieting sight of drawn notched arrows. Small wonder that many converts are made to the movement along the byways and roadsides.

In their intense spiritual darkness, the *Jeunesse* resorted to witchcraft and magic to bolster up their fighting arms and terrorist activities. They boasted of potent arrows specially treated to impart extraordinary powers; they spoke of diminutive planes which transported their leaders instantaneously to any destination desired; they claimed that their leaders had *phonees* (telephones) by means of which they could talk with anyone at any time; they vainly exaggerated their ability to travel hundreds of miles in one night; they confidently declared that the enemy's bullets would turn to water and would be powerless to harm them; and to Mulele Pierre they attributed supernatural powers, which would enable him to make himself invisible or change himself and those with him into palm trees when the enemy approached. (The fact that hundreds of *Jeunesse* have already been mowed down by enemy machine guns must have weakened if not shattered their beliefs in their own invulnerability.)

It is a grievous thought that among the *Jeunesse* there were those whom we loved and taught at our mission schools. Without a doubt, some identified themselves with the movement in all good faith, feeling that it was a legitimate protest directed toward political reform in a corrupt and inept government. But now that the missionaries too were considered enemies and the destruction had struck their own mission stations and schools, they were confused and in doubt. Mr. Bertsche writes:

> During the 48 hours we waited at Kandala to be evacuated person after person sought us out only to stand, gripping our hands, with tears in their eyes, dismay and bewilderment etched in their faces. They would say: "This isn't what was supposed to happen. We weren't told it would be like this."

This I know, there can be no fellowship, no peaceful coexistence, between light and darkness. The division is as marked as day and night! All of us were once in darkness, but God has

"... rescued us out of the darkness and gloom of Satan's

kingdom and brought us into the kingdom of His dear Son"—the kingdom of Light. Colossians 1:13, *Living Letters.*

This He did for the church in Congo and now He commands them and us by our behavior to show that our hearts, once filled with darkness, now are full of light in the Lord. Because of His light within, we have been admonished to do only that which is good and right and true. The Christians who involuntarily and unwittingly had been pulled into the net were faced with a crucial decision. Either they must go on supporting the movement at the price of their own convictions and fall back into darkness or make a break with it. To break would risk their lives, but gain the shining approval of the Lord Jesus Christ, the Light of the World.

And what of the *Jeunesse* themselves—those who are still in such intense darkness? For them too, there is hope. God, Who said, "Let there be light," can and does dispel the inkiest darkness of the human heart. He still opens blind eyes to behold the light of the Gospel.

In the world the darkness grows more dense. The insidious forces of evil seem to be taking the reins of authority. However, the Christian knows there is no need for frustration and fear. God's sure Word of prophecy, as a light shining in a dark place, has told us centuries ago that it would be thus and He bids us to rejoice for our Redeemer is near—even at the door. When He appears all darkness will be forever dispelled by the brightness of His coming.

> Though the cause of Evil prosper, yet 'tis Truth alone is strong,
>
> . . . .
>
> Truth forever on the scaffold, Wrong forever on the throne,—

Yet that scaffold sways the future, and, behind the dim
   unknown,
Standeth God within the shadow, keeping watch above
   his own.

—from "The Present Crisis" by James Russell Lowell.

12

In the Lions' Den

My God hath sent his angel, and hath shut the lions' mouths, and they have not hurt me.

Daniel 6:22

"Mademoiselle, we think you must go to Idiofa where you can get a plane. We have waited long for the *avion* to come to get you here but none has appeared. We don't want you to get killed here; we want to save your life. Some of us will go with you." The speaker was Zabulon, the teacher.

It was late on Monday afternoon, the third day since that first note was dropped promising to send a helicopter to rescue us. It was hard to understand the reason for the delay. I knew that the missionaries in Scotty's Super Cub, which had flown over the day before, had seen me. They knew that my life was in danger. Then why did they not come for me? And now with painful awareness I realized that my presence was also a threat to the lives of the Congolese Christians and their families who were so valiantly seeking to hide and defend me.

I wondered if I should leave the station when the Word had been so clear: "God is in the midst of her; she shall not be moved." Besides, my physical strength and endurance would hardly be sufficient for that twenty-five-mile trek to Idiofa.

As if reading my thoughts, Zabulon said,

"We will take a bicycle and push you when you get tired and we will travel at night so that the sun will not bother you."

Then he laid five eggs on the table which he said was food for the journey, and left me. Zechariah too excused himself to go to eat. He had sat with me all day and was by now hungry.

I was glad to be left alone for I was disturbed about this new turn of events. I needed a special word of direction from the Lord who alone knows the future. The decision had to be made quickly and I asked for a clear, unmistakable answer, which would leave no doubt as to what I was to do. As I opened my Bible my eyes fell on Genesis 46:3, 4:

"Fear not . . . I will go down with thee." With this, another verse flashed into my mind: "Jesus himself drew near and went with them." A third promise was given not only to assure safety in the way, but also to give confidence of a safe and sure arrival at the place prepared for me:

"Behold, I send an Angel before thee, to keep thee in the way, and to bring thee into the place which I have prepared." Exodus 23:20

An indescribable peace flooded my soul, and when the men returned I was ready with my answer: "Yes, I will go, for the Lord Himself will go with us."

They brought me *luku* and greens to fortify me physically. I had no appetite but knowing that a special portion of strength would be needed for the trip ahead, I ate a few bites—as much as I could swallow.

It was night when Pastor Luka dressed in his large suit coat and, armed with bow and arrow, opened the door of the hut.

"We are ready to go," he announced.

Outside Chief Nzadi and two men from the village were waiting, similarly armed. One man was standing by Luka's bicycle. I recognized him as Madinga, the speedy messenger of Mangungu village who had at times carried urgent messages for us. From everywhere Christians appeared to press my hand silently and whisper,

"*Nzambi lunda nge*" (God keep you).

They vanished again into the darkness. We got into a huddle and once more Luka prayed briefly for the Lord's direction and protection, then led the way out into the night.

We followed the road down into the valley toward the village of Luembe-Nene. Before we reached the river a messenger overtook us. He brought a piece of old plastic for my protection in case of rain, another evidence of loving concern. The bridge had been destroyed and the river was now spanned by a narrow log. I took my shoes off and crossed with bare feet, slowly sliding the right foot forward and dragging the left foot after it, thus managing to keep both feet on the log. On the other side of the water we had to detour around a deep trench dug across the road, which had been cleverly camouflaged by sticks and grass. The *Jeunesse* had done all they could to cut off any possible way of escape by vehicle and to prevent reprisal by the soldiers.

At the top of the hill as we entered Luembe-Nene we were met by Zechariah, Samuel, and Zabulon, also armed. Together we walked on to the chapel where some of the Christian women were waiting for us. There followed a whispered discussion as to the best way of procedure. There were two possible routes to Idiofa. One was little more than a footpath through the grassy plains; the other was the open road usually traveled from Luembe. The risk of meeting bands of *Jeunesse* seemed equally great on both routes. Their choice fell to the main highway.

Before leaving, Luka and Zechariah, the two godly pastors who often shared problems and counseled together, had a brief and secret consultation. Together they went into Zechariah's house. When they returned after a few moments, Luka handed me fifteen hundred francs (about five dollars).

"This is from both churches for your plane trip to Kikwit," he explained. "We know you have nothing left and you will need this to get out."

I was deeply moved by their thoughtfulness and generosity. Like the Macedonian church, in the midst of their own ordeal of severe trial and affliction, out of their depth of poverty had overflowed a wealth of lavish generosity on their part. They were giving not only what they could afford but far more, and they were doing it voluntarily from a deep desire to help their sister in Christ. Never before had I been reduced to such poverty that I needed financial help from my poor Congolese brethren, but never before had a gift meant quite so much to me. I felt rich in my poverty as I thanked Luka and handed the money back to him, asking him to put it in his inside coat pocket for safe keeping. His ample outside pocket had already become the receptacle for the five eggs.

The moon was coming up when the procession, joined now by Zechariah and his brother, once more took the road for Idiofa. We traveled in silence—six armed men, with Madinga walking beside me pushing the bicycle. Contentedly I thoughtfully pondered the words: *Fear not, I will go down with thee. . . . Jesus himself drew near and went with them.* The exquisite beauty of the silvery moonlight shimmered upon the palm trees along the way. At the foot of a long hill there was another river, a wider and deeper one this time. The bridge was gone, but again I crossed successfully on the log in my bare feet. Long and arduous was the climb up the hill on the other side. I was grateful when Madinga stepped by my side with the bicycle.

"Get on, Mademoiselle, I'll push you a while."

Noiselessly we proceeded on our way. Only the faint swish of Nzadi's stiff loincloth as he strode along and the heavy breathing of Madinga as he pushed the bicycle could be heard. There were very faint whisperings, too, among my escorts. I could barely detect the subject of their apprehension: a single Congolese with bow and arrow who had previously met us on the road. He had assured us that everything was all right ahead, but now the men were becoming uneasy as to whether he was foe or friend. I spoke to no one; no one spoke to me.

"*Telema!*" Like a sudden thunderclap a voice commanded us to halt. Armed terrorists sprang from the grass on both sides of the road. It took only a startled moment to see we had been ambushed.

"Where are you going? Why are you traveling at night?" they demanded roughly.

Luka tried to explain that they were taking me to Idiofa to get the plane from there to Kikwit. There was much noisy parleying and confusion.

"Kill her, kill her!" they clamored.

"Let's take her to the president," one said as he grabbed me by the arm and started pulling me into the grass.

Instantly Zechariah was by my side. With my free hand I grabbed his arm. Somehow I had the strength to hold on. I asserted almost pleadingly,

"If I go, Zechariah will go with me." Amazingly, and to my astonishment, the terrorist released me.

"*Beto kwenda*" (Let us go), Zechariah said simply.

We made our way down the grassy path accompanied by the gang of *Jeunesse*—in front, behind, to the left and to the right—scores of them forming the circumference of an imprisoning circle. One who claimed the title of secretary walked beside me.

"Don't you know that it is against our law to travel at night? We could kill you," he said threateningly, "but first we will take you to the president and see what punishment he will order for you."

Fear not, I will go down with thee. This was the promise of the Friend that sticketh closer than a brother, and I knew He was with us right now. To the secretary I said,

"God is with me. He is right here with us now, and He

loves you too. He gave His Son, Jesus, to die for you and He wants to save you."

"If you talk like that, we will surely kill you," snarled a wicked voice behind me. "Look out, there's an arrow aimed at your back; someone is going to shoot you!" I knew this was meant to frighten me. I did not even look around but continued talking to the secretary about my Savior—Who wanted to be his, if he would but accept Him.

There ensued the typically loud discussion in their tribal tongue as we walked what seemed a long distance through the grass. The number of the *Jeunesse* kept increasing as we went along. Finally we came to the gate of the pole fence in front of the president's house. Here we halted. He came out to give me an authoritative lecture about breaking the rules of traveling at night. Then he added,

"You are lucky that I had my sentries out to capture you. There is a much fiercer *equipe* [group] guarding the road ahead. They are strangers here and they would have killed you without question. We are showing you mercy because we know you."

There followed another of those interminable long and strident discussions as to what to do with us and how to punish us. There were more threats on my life. Some of their talk was in Kituba, the language I understood; this was for my benefit, I suppose. Someone suggested that they put me into their *boloko* (prison) for the rest of the night; someone else that they give all of us the "water" punishment, and a third that we be made to stand guard outside until morning. Through all the Lord gave me a peace and a calm not of myself. I knew He was there and had the situation well in hand.

In the end we were all admitted into the president's house. He showed me a canvas-backed chair.

"*Vanda*" (sit), he said.

I dropped into it exhausted. Closing my eyes, I thanked the Lord for the reality of His presence with me and reminded Him of His promise to keep me in the way and to bring me to the place which He had prepared for me. I knew not where this prepared place was nor how to get there, but wherever or however, I trusted Him to fulfill His promise in His time.

"Mademoiselle! Mademoiselle!" a rasping voice barked at my side. I opened my eyes to see a man with a cruel face staring at me. He had a honed knife in his right hand and was wiping the blade with the fingers of his left hand. "I'm getting this ready to cut your throat!" he hissed.

"I'm not afraid to die," I said, "for I know where I am going."

"Not afraid to die?" he queried in astonishment. "What kind of a Mademoiselle are you? If you are not afraid to die, I'd better kill you."

"Although I'm not *afraid* to die, I don't want to die," I said. "We all want to live until the Lord calls us Home." Then I spoke to him of the Savior's love, of the One Who died on the cross to take away our sins and give us eternal life and Who alone can deliver from the fear of death. Again I saw the miracle happen. His hard, cruel face softened and he drew back.

Meanwhile the room had filled with curious, clamoring *Jeunesse.*

"*Bima! bima! bima!*"

It was the same terrifying cry as that night they first attacked Irene and me. Most of them were young men in their late teens or early twenties. I thought I recognized among them some of the faces of former school children at the mission.

Now it was the secretary's turn to take over. He ordered

me to dump the contents of my little bag on the floor. One by one he carefully examined each article as he handled it. There were many onlookers.

"Those village people have made the Mademoiselle very poor," was the dry comment.

The secretary then produced paper and a ballpoint pen. Handing it to me he said,

"Write down just what I tell you."

He dictated as I wrote: "We were captured because we disobeyed the rules and traveled at night. We were not harmed."

Then he had me make a list of all the articles in the bag as he named them off: a cake of soap, a washcloth, a comb, a Bible, *Daily Light*, etc. They found the fifteen hundred francs in Luka's pocket and this, too, had to be put on the list.

Then he asked, "Do you have your signature anywhere?"

I showed him my Bible in which I had written my name.

"I want you to sign this statement just that same way," he commanded. This I did, and then he said, with determination,

"Now, Mademoiselle, we want to know *where* your telephone is." I assured them that I had no telephone. (I did of course have an invisible "phone" which gave me direct and immediate connections to Heaven—to the Father's ear. Even a thought, a desire, a longing, a groan which could not be uttered were heard by Him.) Evidently my bag held nothing of value to them for he told me to put the items back and then returned it to me.

Though the head president or commandant was nowhere in evidence, there were a number of things that gave me strong reason to suspect that I was in the hands of the same gang that had made the attack on our mission at Mangungu.

"Who killed your friend?" they asked defiantly.

"I don't know. It was dark and I couldn't see who it was," I answered.

"But who killed her?" they persisted.

"God only knows who he was," I replied.

"It's the village people who did it," they insisted.

I was certain it was a member of the *Jeunesse* who had killed Irene. I was afraid they wanted me to say so and thus incriminate myself by accusing them; but I knew it would be folly to do this. It was best to evade the question, let them tell the lies, and then let them proceed to interrogate me about other matters if they wished.

"Where did you hide all your money?" they wanted to know next.

I knew that after paying the workmen, students, and nurses there was very little money left in my purse—perhaps ten dollars or less. Irene, on the contrary, had quite a large sum of money in her purse. We shared all station expenses, but since we had no time on Friday evening to settle accounts between us, we left that to do on the way out. So I could understand their surprise to find so little cash in my bag. I did, however, have two fifty-dollar checks from home, and it was doubtless because of these that the secretary was so insistent to get my exact signature.

Then the president said,

"We have already captured Idiofa and will soon have all of the Kwilu province. We are going to attack Kikwit next. Tonight some of our men are making an assault on Yassa Lokwa [the sector post nearest to Mangungu where a contingent of soldiers and government officials were stationed]. When we are rid of the soldiers and officials there, we will have the entire district under our control."

Then came the question, "What are you? Where is your country?"

"I am an American," I answered.

"We do not like America. You are no longer American; from now on you are P.S.A. (*Parti Solidaire Africain*). You are one of us," they said with finality. "You will never be able to get to your country without your passport."

Again the promise flashed into my mind, *I will send my Angel to keep thee in the way and to bring thee to the place which I have prepared for thee.* Could it be that His "prepared place" was right here among the rebels, to be a witness for Him, to point them to the Light of Life?

By now it must have been far past midnight and I was very tired. Seeing my weariness the president said with some concern,

"Mademoiselle, you are tired. We will prepare a place for you to lie down and rest."

After dismissing his men, he led me to a small bedroom in the back of the house. In it was a bamboo bed covered with a native blanket.

"You will be safe here," he said. "Have no fear; no one will molest you."

Then he closed the door and I was alone. For some time I could hear voices outside, but gradually all became quiet.

Shortly I heard the splatter of rain running off the grass roof. I was thankful to be under the shelter of the president's roof rather than out on the road to Idiofa. Lying there on the bamboo bed, I relived the events of the past hours. I felt a kinship to the prophet Daniel when he was thrown into the lions' den for I, too, had been in a den of lions, but God had sent His angels to shut their mouths, and they had not hurt me. I felt at peace and was soon sound asleep.

13
The Snare Is Broken

*If it had not been the Lord who was on our
side, when men rose up against us: Then
they had swallowed us up quick. . . . Our
soul is escaped as a bird out of the snare of
the fowlers: the snare is broken, and we are
escaped.*

Psalm 124:2, 3, 7

Day was dawning when I awoke somewhat refreshed. With half-open eyes and hazy remembrance I viewed the strange room about me. As consciousness returned, I realized I was in the *Jeunesse* president's house. I recapitulated the events of the past four days: There had been the appearance of the missionary plane and its messages, the hasty but incomplete preparations for evacuation, the night attack on our house, Irene's murder, the nasty wound in my left arm still in its original bandage, the bed of cracked wheat in the garage, the preparation of Irene's body for burial, the raucous noise of hacking and looting, the first harrowing lonely moments in the dispensary, and then the glorious sense of the presence of God following the thunderstorm.

Later had come the medical hut-hopping to hide from pursuing *Jeunesse,* the crouching in the grass like a frightened animal, the threat of a honed knife, the hospitality of Luka's non-Christian uncle, the percussion of running feet, soft whispered consultations, occasional outbursts of loud discussions, the miracles of protection, and our arduous trek to Idiofa. Dotting the kaleidoscopic scenes were the evidences of God's faithfulness in the perfect, apt Scripture verse for each occasion, the innumerable little thoughtful kindnesses of my Congolese Christian friends and the brave exposures of their lives—especially Pastor Luka and Pastor Zechariah. I thought of last night's verdict by my captors:

"You are no longer an American; you are one of us!"
and I wondered what the new day held in store for me.

I opened my *Daily Light* to the morning reading of January 28:

"As thy days, so shall thy strength be. . . . He giveth

power to the faint, and to them that have no might He increaseth strength. . . . My grace is sufficient for thee for my strength is made perfect in weakness."

Whatever the exigencies of the day, I was assured of strength and power and grace to meet them victoriously. There was further admonition,

"Take no thought for the morrow. . . . Sufficient unto the day is the evil thereof."

I found comfort in the certainty that I had to live but one day at a time and my tomorrows were safe in God's keeping. After such spiritual refreshment and encouragement, I opened the door of my unusual host's house and stepped outside. As I looked around, to my amazement I saw that I was actually in the village of Kimpata. I had thought we were in some deep forest hideout, although I had been somewhat puzzled about the size and structure of the president's house. The fact that they were now out in the open bore eloquent testimony to the rapid and complete takeover by the *Jeunesse*. No longer was it necessary for them to carry on in secret forest hideouts. They were now in possession of the entire village.

My escorts from Mangungu and Luembe were there also; only Chief Nzadi was missing for he had made his escape when we were ambushed. All had been disarmed the night before. Pastor Luka, because he was recognized as the leader of the group, suffered a few sharp slaps across the face on the false charges of having stolen from the mission. My heart went out to him and I prayed that he and the other faithful believers might know the blessedness promised to those who would be reviled, persecuted, and falsely accused for Christ's sake. I desired that they might be given grace to rejoice and be exceedingly glad, to be counted worthy to suffer for Christ's sake.

For breakfast the *Jeunesse* brought me some boiled eggs—

from the supply in Luka's coat pocket—and *luku*. While I was eating, Muke, a village Christian, came with a few grains of salt, a most precious and hard-to-get staple, to make the eggs more savory. How much these little kindnesses meant!

After breakfast the president came to talk with me.

"It is impossible for you to get to Idiofa now, Mademoiselle," he said. "We are going to take you back to Mangungu. Meanwhile we will prepare for you here and will get you again tomorrow morning."

This decision surprised me, but I was extremely grateful for .it. The Lord Himself had moved the heart of this leader, for

"The king's heart is in the hand of the Lord, as the rivers of water: he turneth it whithersoever he will." Proverbs 21:1.

"I myself will accompany you with some of my men to make sure that you arrive safely," he continued.

The sun was already high in the heavens when we left the village. The president and his men went ahead. Close to me with bow and arrow in hand walked Mukidi, the man in whose house Irene and I had stayed on our two week-end trips to Kimpata. He had joined himself to the *Jeunesse* but was now serving as my bodyguard and protector and I was glad for his presence. Madinga, bicycle in tow, also accompanied our heterogeneous caravan.

The atmosphere was charged with tension. Armed men popped out from the grass everywhere, and repeatedly we were commanded to halt. Sentries had been set up all along the road and on every footpath to control all traffic and communication. Every traveler was ordered to halt and stand at attention. I learned later that if, after the third bidding, anyone refused to obey, the sentry had authority to shoot to kill without further ado. As our procession moved slowly along, punctuated at intervals with extended halts and explanations by Mukidi, I was deeply impressed with the utter impossibility of making an escape by land. The only way left now was to be air-lifted. But I knew too that the *Jeunesse* had determined not to let any plane land for me, and that any attempt to rescue me by air might result in a massacre.

After plodding wearily on toward Mangungu for an hour or more, the president who had been far in the lead, met us on his way back. He said,

"I am returning now, but some of my men will remain with you to see that you arrive safely. Tomorrow morning we will come for you. *Bika mbote* (Farewell)."

Judging from the position of the sun, I deduced it was almost noon when we approached Luembe-Nene. The sun was beating down upon us mercilessly and I was dragging, scarcely able to put one foot ahead of the other. But God's Word that morning had been: *As thy days, so shall thy strength be. . . . He giveth power to the faint, and to them that have no might He increaseth strength.* Madinga, still pushing the bicycle, stopped beside me. He noticed my weariness.

"Mademoiselle, sit on the crossbar; I will carry you," he said solicitously. I gladly complied and we continued on our sweltering way.

We found the village of Luembe-Nene alive with armed men milling around in the clearing near the road. Shortly I discovered the reason for their agitation: the buzzing of a plane to the right of us. Looking up, I saw the MAF Cessna coming from the direction of Mangungu. I knew they had been looking for me and were now flying back without any knowledge of my whereabouts. Desperately I waved but they were too far away and there was no answering dip or tilt to indicate that they had seen me. The handful of *Jeun-*

esse still with us made no effort to stop my signal. They knew the plane had not seen me. I gazed longingly and with heavy heart as they flew completely from view, disappearing in the southern sky.

Now my last hope of escape was gone. Utterly forlorn, I dejectedly sat down on a log by the side of the road and, putting my head in my hands, was oblivious to all about me. If only the plane had come an hour later I would have been there. Then at least they would have known that I was still alive. However, if the attempt to rescue me would mean more bloodshed, it was best so. Yes, Lord, Thy grace is sufficient for me—sufficient for any eventuality of the future, even if this meant remaining among the terrorists as a witness to His all-sufficiency.

Little did I guess that the very fact I was not seen by the MAF served to hasten rescue operations. At that very moment the pilot, Wes Eisemann, was flashing a message to Tshikapa to Colonel Meyer, commander of the UN rescue operations:

> Signaled to land at Mangungu. Hege apparently ill. Did not come out-of-doors. No sign of activity in area.

"Let us go on, Mademoiselle." It was Luka's voice gently urging me to press on, for we had not yet reached our destination.

I felt faint and withered like the parched grass from the terrific heat of the tropical noonday sun, but *He giveth power to the faint.* I needed it now, this very moment, and true to His promise, it was given without delay. I got up from my bleak musing and followed along the road toward the once-peaceful mission compound.

Upon our arrival at Mangungu the Christians were

amazed and surprised to see us. They told us of the circling
of the MAF plane and how they had signaled that I had
gone to Idiofa. This only added to the confusion in my
thinking, but to the invisible Director of this rescue operation, there was perfect order and timing.

Wes Eisemann wrote later:

> In order to hurry the U.N. helicopters we purposely
> went to Tshikapa to talk to Colonel Meyer. We knew
> that you had been injured but did not know how seri-
> ously. So we were becoming more and more anxious
> to get you evacuated. . . .
>
> The U.N. wanted proof that you were still there at
> Mangungu and still in need of evacuation. We were
> to overfly your station again and radio back our find-
> ings to Colonel Meyer. We flew over Mangungu
> about 11:30 and noticed no one on the station itself.
> . . . After circling for the third time we noticed a
> couple of men north of the station signaling as though
> they wanted me to land. They brought their arms
> down from over their heads to the ground. They also
> pointed to what I thought was a building where you
> were located. I assumed from this that you were very
> ill and needed to be evacuated right away. I radioed
> the message to Colonel Meyer.

To me who could see only one minute part of the whole
operation, the snare of the fowler seemed to be closing in
on every side. However, the Almighty God was timing
the movements with omnipotent precision and was causing
all things to dovetail into the perfect working out of His
plan.

The mission, deserted an hour earlier when the MAF

plane flew over, was suddenly once again alive with *Jeun-esse* who had followed me. Luka led me through the station by a back path to the far end of Mangungu village where his brother had a large mud-and-pole house. They brought out a chair for me and put it under the spreading mango tree in the back yard. I felt that I had reached the end of my strength and could not go another step so I was thankful to sit down and relax in the cool refreshing shade. Several members of the *Jeunesse*, whom I had not seen before, came to take note of where I was resting. They did not guard me closely now for they were confident that all means of escape by land were closed. I could see my Volkswagen hidden under some palm branches just a little distance from where I was sitting. It made me feel good to know that the little car that had served us so faithfully in the past was still unharmed.

After all my visitors had withdrawn, Luka took me to a small house in the back, which was used for a storeroom. This was to be my hiding place for the present. I noticed the back door of our house, which had been dismantled by the looters, one of our kitchen chairs, and some other familiar household articles in the room. Luka once more brought my cot bed to me. There was just space enough inside from wall to wall to set it up.

It was now Tuesday afternoon, three and a half days since the initial *Jeunesse* attack. My shoulder wound had not been dressed since Saturday so Luka went through the village to hunt for iodine and bandage. In a little while Jakob, who had previously worked in a dispensary, but had been dismissed for some unknown reason, appeared with a bottle of the white alcohol we had guarded jealously in our pharmacy. With considerable flourish, to display his medical skill, no doubt, he took off the dirty bandage, cleaned the wound with alcohol and iodine, and bound it again with a clean bandage. I gasped when afterward I saw him cup his palm, fill it with alcohol, and proceed to wash his hands in the precious liquid. Doubtless he had seen the doctors in the hospital do this after scrubbing up. However, I said nothing to him about this extravagant waste, but thanked him for his kindness in so efficiently dressing my wound.

To quench my thirst, Marcelene brought me a bottle of boiled water, which she had taken from my refrigerator. She also brought me a ripe papaya. I thanked God and ate and drank and felt refreshed. Some of the village women came in to greet me, bringing gifts of pineapple and eggs. I talked to them of the Lord and his lovingkindness to me and to them, and we were mutually encouraged.

When I was once again left alone, I stretched out on my cot for a rest. Suddenly I heard the dissonance of a multitude of voices and then the confused pounding of many running feet. Startled, I sat up at the thought that the terrorists were hunting me again. However, to my relief, they did not stop but continued past the large house, quite unaware of the little storeroom in the rear that was sheltering me. For some time the talking, running, and excitement continued; then all was quiet once more.

After a short lapse of time Marcelene came in to visit me again. I asked her about the disturbance. She told me that the news had gone out through the village that some of the National soldiers from Yassa Lokwa (where the *Jeunesse* had made the attack the night before) had escaped to the forest. Their supply of ammunition was exhausted so all the men in the village, including the *Jeunesse*, were out to hunt and kill the hated soldiers. Though I felt deeply sorry for the trapped army, it was good to have the village cleared of *Jeunesse* at least for a few hours. I again lay down and relaxed.

I can't say what my thoughts were then. I was tired physically, exhausted emotionally, but at peace spiritually. I do know my ears were constantly alert and attuned to catch the sound I longed most to hear, even as I lay back and rested.

And then, seemingly out of the blue, came a faint drone. The drone grew louder and louder until it swelled into the most beautiful and thrilling crescendo I could imagine. I sprang to my feet, dashed out of doors, and looked up. A plane bearing the initials ONU (United Nations) was approaching. They were coming to rescue me! I must get to the clearing on the station, and I must get there quickly. As the drone increased to a roar I saw not only the UN plane, but two UN helicopters following.

Without returning to the hut for my bag, I ran into the village street.

"*Velo, Velo!*" (bicycle), I called urgently.

Not a vehicle was in sight. I had no strength left to run. Two older village men were standing, looking on with interest. I grabbed them by the arm, one on each side of me, and shouted,

"Pull me! Run with me! I must get there!" But they were too startled and too old to run fast. It was a long way to the clearing on the mission where the pilots would be able to see me. At the rate we were going we would not get there in time, for already the plane was out of sight, buzzing the station.

Then from I know not where a young man appeared with a bicycle. I recognized him as a village man, but not a professing Christian. God bless him!

"Get on!" he yelled. I jumped on the crossbar and he pedaled full speed down the village street toward the mission. We passed a man with bow and arrow in readiness. My "chauffeur" said reassuringly,

"*Tita ve* (Don't fear). He can't hurt you."

As we neared the clearing the planes were making the second circle around.

"Wave, Mademoiselle!" ordered my conductor. I clung to the speeding bicycle with my left hand and waved my right into the air. There in front of the medical huts were Luka and Akiem motioning the planes down.

"Come, Mademoiselle, come," they urged.

Jumping from the bike, I staggered toward the helicopter coming down behind the medical chapel, while the other hovered in mid-air. I stumbled through the grass. The helicopter touched ground. The lieutenant leaped out, ran to meet me, took my arm, and helped me into the 'copter. I collapsed on the seat.

In a moment we were air-borne.

Because the Lord was on my side, the fowlers' snare was broken and I had escaped.

14
Epilogue

(in collaboration with K. Boerwinkle)

> " . . . *You are very dear to me. For during the time I was in bonds, as well as when I was out defending and demonstrating the power of the Gospel, we shared together the grace of God. Only God knows how deep is my love and longing for you* . . . "
>
> Philippians 1:7,8

July 1973 — nine and a half years after the two United Nations helicopters effected my rescue from the *Jeunesse* — I was airborne again. Through those years since my helicopter rescue on that fateful January 28th, 1964, my blessed Lord was continually my protection and refuge.

Now, in stark contrast, I was at Kennedy Airport on a very hot first-of-July night, 1973. In place of the odd collection of assorted clothing I wore for my homecoming in 1964, I was neatly dressed in my own well-fitting clothes. Instead of exhaustion, dismay, and the bewilderment of having to run for my life, I was leisurely embarking on a modern, air-conditioned, 747 jumbo jet and anticipating a warm reunion with my faithful, beloved brothers and sisters in Christ in the Kwilu Province — especially those at Mangungu Station.

Following an uneventful takeoff of the 747 I settled back into my comfortable reserved seat to relax and enjoy the flight across the Atlantic. But my busy mind would not relax. It raced ahead excitedly. We were only 15 hours — airtime — from the land of my first love, the Congo! The Congo? No, there was no more Congo. That name connoted the Old Belgian colonialism — it was Zaire now and my airline ticket read, "Republique du Zaire." Just exactly what was involved in this change I was not totally aware, but with discipline and practice that new name would be fixed in my mind and it would slip easily from my tongue.

Back in 1964 political uncertainties prevented my soon return to Congo. The first order of business, upon reaching the States following rescue, was my physical, emotional and spiritual recuperation. There were days of earnest prayer and fasting for those dear Congolese who had risked their very lives to assure my safety and ultimate rescue. Thoughts of them and their probable, but un-

196 • We Two Alone

known, suffering often interrupted whatever I happened
to be doing day or night and prompted intercession for
them at the Throne of Grace. The Lord long ago taught
this servant that those early morning wakeful hours, when
households are quiet, are excellent times to read His Word
and meet Him for uninterrupted communion. In God's
marvelous mercy and grace He kept me from the agony of
terrifying nightmares one might expect would follow the
attack and pursuit of the *Jeunesse.*

Three months of rest, loving care of my family and close
friends, and good food had begun to restore some of my
spent energies. Reporters were regularly storming the
door for interviews; radio stations were asking for tapes
or personal appearances; magazines — Christian and sec-
ular — sought exclusive stories of my experience; book
publishers were vying for a book relating those January
days; churches wanted me to speak and tell my story;
there was even the bid to make a movie.

Through the good help and intervention of my sister and
the counsel of men at the home office of Baptist Mid-
Missions, I was spared many difficult encounters with
curiosity seekers. My younger sister, Marie, had a firm
and effective "No."

Invitations to speak were literally piled high. Everywhere I turned there were decisions to make, letters to
write, phone calls to answer, people to see. Instead of the
relatively quiet furlough of a missionary home from the
field, I was suddenly swept up into the hectic pace of a
celebrity. But I wasn't a celebrity. I longed for the quiet
of the mission field — at least the quiet that was ours until
the attack of the *Jeunesse.* However, the Lord had His
plans — "For I know the thoughts that I think toward
you ... thoughts of peace, and not of evil ... " (Jeremiah
29:11). He had spared me that I might have the privilege

of sharing with others His goodness and power — not for any glory of my own, but for His glory. Thus began the thousands of miles of travel, the seemingly endless speaking engagements, the laborious hours of writing, editing, and rewriting of *We Two Alone*, answering the steady stream of letters and phone calls, and attending luncheons and dinners lovingly prepared in my honor.

The Lord taught me how to relate His Word and His working in the Congo so that I was not completely spent emotionally after each public message. He was pleased to use His Word to speak to hearts. Youthful lives were dedicated for the first time to follow wherever He should lead. Cold hearts were drawn back to the warmth of a close walk with their Lord. Some have in these nine and a half years finished their training and gone on to serve on the mission fields of the world. Were these trophies worth Irene's death? Were these worth the harrassment and suffering of those dear Congolese I left behind when I entered the UN helicopter? And what about the prisoner who read *We Two Alone* in his cell in the Michigan State Penitentiary? Was his salvation worth such cost? Only eternity will reveal the harvest that was reaped from the grain of wheat which fell into the ground in Congo (John 12:24).

We Two Alone was published March 1, 1965 in time to take one last long speaking tour before leaving for Costa Rica. Baptist Mid-Missions missionaries on the Venezuelan field extended a warm and unanimous invitation to come back to work with them when they learned the Congo was closed to me. As I prayed over their invitation the Lord spoke to me saying, "This is the way, walk ye in it."

After a short refresher course in a Costa Rica Spanish language school, I enplaned for Caracas and Puerto Ordaz. The Venezuelan churches welcomed my return with the warmth and affection peculiarly theirs.

There was time for two additional terms of service before retirement from the mission. During the first of those terms *We Two Alone* was published in Spanish at the request of my Venezuelan brethren. Again the Lord was pleased to touch hearts through the messages from His Word and the simple testimony of His loving care as I spoke in the churches and damas' (ladies) meetings.

As the second term progressed I reluctantly faced the hard fact of my speedy approach to the Biblical quota of "three score years and ten." After 40 blessed years of service on two foreign soils, not to return to the kind of work I loved seemed unthinkable. Inwardly I rebelled; but graciously, patiently the Lord taught me that how or where I serve Him is not for me to determine. Only the doing of His will is important to the servant. Back in the States again I found peace and realized a sense of joyous anticipation as I approached and entered unexpected and newly-opened doors. I did not lack service for the Lord! I was busier than ever for my calendar was filled with speaking engagements in many states. When I was home in Wellington I also found there was much to do.

News from the bush in Congo was meager and often depressing. They wrote, "Mamma Hege, why don't you come back? You told us when you were here about the Apostle Paul who visited his churches. Can't *you* visit us? We know he wrote to some of his churches ... Mamma Hege, will you write to us again? We miss you. Why don't you come back?"

They did not tell me much about themselves nor what they were doing, but I sensed an urgency in their meager messages. Until now, 1973, it was not feasible, nor had the mission council encouraged me, to return to Africa. But deep within there was a constant longing to go back, to see for myself what had occurred in my absence. Were the churches still healthy and growing? What had my friends suffered because they dared to help me in my flight from the *Jeunesse*? Unanswered questions tumbled over each other whenever I thought at any length of Mangungu Station.

In the midst of the newly opened doors of service in my stateside retirement God said, "It is time now for you to return to the land of your first love." He lovingly provided the funds and did the exceeding abundant by adding a delightful traveling companion and here we sat side by side·on this great 747 jet en route to Africa! Sound asleep in the next seat was Katie Boerwinkle, a long-time faithful friend. She had followed me with prayerful interest all the years of my missionary service.

Try as I might my mind kept jumping the miles thinking of this one or that, pondering what had happened recently to the few co-laborers who were permitted to return to Zaire when the unrest had abated sufficiently to assure their safety.

In the spring of 1973 all our Baptist Mid-Missions missionaries were asked to terminate their work in Zaire. The official document proposed by the leaders of the Church of Christ in Zaire dealing with the subject of "Authentic Christians in the Zairian Policy of Authenticity" was carefully scrutinized by the mission council. The entire matter was discussed and prayerfully considered before the mission Home Council deemed it Biblically impossible to cooperate with the Zairian ecumenical doctrinaire.

By July 1973 one BMM missionary family, the Bob Grings, remained on the field along with one single missionary, Ruth Yost. It was Bob and Winnie Grings in whose home we were to stay. It was upon them we would be dependent for food and transportation. We were aware the Zairian roads were indescribably bad, but by whatever means the Grings had found best for travel we would also travel.

My heart warmed as I thought of Winnie, who had adopted me as her older sister after Irene's death: unselfish, resourceful, gentle, patient, practical Winnie. Her welcome smile would belie the heartache or discouragement through which she most surely had been passing.

Then I thought of Bob. Probably he would leave meeting the plane to Winnie. Faithful to his calling, he would be occupied serving the nationals. Likely he would be busy distributing gospel literature and tapes received from August Eicher and recharging batteries for the tape recorders. *Munganga* (doctor) and Mrs. Eicher found it necessary because of their age, after his eye surgery, to retire in their native Switzerland. Their burning desire to continue to evangelize the unsaved and minister to the converts in Kwilu Province was still glowing. *Munganga's* joy since his retirement is producing gospel tapes in the French, Kituba, and Kiwango and then air mailing them to Bob. Through these tapes Bob was maintaining an itinerant ministry out in the bush and had devised his own method of keeping the recorder batteries charged.

Missionaries may be forced to relocate, but they do not forget the people and lands they leave behind. Like Peter, they continue to feed the flock of God "so that they may never stumble or fall away." I'm sure dear Brother Eicher identifies closely with the aged apostle who wrote to his believers, "As long as I am still here I intend to keep sending these reminders to you hoping to impress them so clearly upon you that you will remember long after I have gone" II Peter 1:14, 15.

How perfectly the Lord led Bob Grings and August

Eicher, each talented in such different ways and separated by some 5000 miles, to synchronize their diverse gifts in order to sustain the national Christians spiritually.

From Bob my thoughts moved to Becky and Danny Grings. When I saw them last they were happy youngsters full of fun and tricks. In general both were obedient and respectful, fluent in the national tongue, lovers of the outdoors, pets, and African children. I had heard that they attended a year or two of public school in the States while on furlough. They had lived on Grandfather Ferrel's farm in Idaho where they helped with the daily chores and enjoyed horseback riding. How had exposure to American youth and living affected their unspoiled lives? Would they be rebellious? sullen? perhaps shy? How would they dress? By now both were teenagers and while they might be far from the direct influence of American youth, they could read, and certainly they corresponded with their peers in America. It would be interesting to see how they had developed.

Then I remembered Ruthie Yost. That petite, dedicated youthful Ruthie was most capable as a teacher and confidante. She was unusually gifted in French; and she was still on the field by permission of the Council completing her term as directress of the government secondary school at Idiofa.

And what of the faithful pastors who helped me escape — Luka and Zechariah? There was such spotty information. They had suffered — that I knew. But in what ways or to what extent I didn't know. God willing, I would soon meet them face to face; I would hear from their own lips what had happened to them. The unknown bicycle pedaller who sped me that last distance down the village street to the mission station and the clearing — Lord, what of him? Would I see him and learn his identity? Would he be a

Christian now? Other faces came to mind, too, but I was growing weary. I closed my eyes and soon joined my seat mate in sleep.

* * * * * * *

Excitement mounted as we approached Kinshasa airfield. Arrival was uneventful except for the loss of my International Health Certificate. In Zaire this document is as important as a passport or visa. Somehow it disappeared from the hands of Bundo, the most trusted representative of Menno Travel Agency. By previous arrangement he met us at the plane and processed our visas and luggage. Without a health certificate how could we possibly proceed to Idiofa the next day? Sleepless, dismayed, and unnerved, I was gently reminded of God's promise given me three months before, "Don't worry about a thing, my child. I will handle all the details" (Ruth 3:11, *Living Bible*).

Of course He would handle all the details — and He did. Impossible as it still seems to me, the ever present armored guard was blinded or his ears were stopped as I smiled, showed him my vaccination scar, and offered my explanation in halting Kituba. The uniformed officer at the little Ndola airport on the outskirts of Kinshasa said, "Ça va!" and waved me on. Luck? No! God's promise to me was that He would "handle all the details" and thus He did for the entire month of travel inside and out of Zaire.

Our flight from Ndola to Idiofa was made in an ancient twelve-seat prop plane whose four rear seats had to be removed to make room for the luggage. Departure was happily only two and a half hours late. The smell of the plane was almost overpowering; the engine was noisy, vibrating, and a bit frightening, but we were spellbound as we looked down on rolling hills and mountains, thick forests, tall grasses and bush country. There was something of a thrill as we landed and took off at the "whistle stops" that were tiny grass-covered runways with airport offices in ramshackle lean-tos.

Our pilot at last announced, "Idiofa." There below us was Winnie, beaming and vigorously waving from the pick-up truck. That four-wheel-drive Jeep truck was to be our sole, but sure means of transportation.

We had our initiation in Zairian road engineering as we traveled to the Grings' home in Kifwanzondo. The Republic of Zaire had not been able to train sufficient national civil engineers to replace the Belgian contingent forced to leave after Independence. The result was hazardous roads characterized by corrugated, rocky, lopsided, dusty ruts often moving in unexpected directions. Instead of curving around the mountains as the Belgians had built them, many roads are straight up and down the mountains! Viewing those jutted rocks, slides, precipitous edges and chasms I realized my trusty little VW, so carefully hidden from the attackers years ago, would never have survived these obstacles. Bob's 1964 Jeep carefully repaired and serviced regularly by his deft hands under direction of his mechanical knowledge seemed up to every challenge.

It was dark when we arrived at Kifwanzondo. We were greeted by a group of clamoring nationals and later by Bob himself who had just come home from an evangelization-shopping tour in Kikwit. Between trips when on the station, Bob could most often be found under a truck, his own or a national's, fitting a worn engine with parts he himself had fashioned from odds and ends. There was no auto-parts store on which to call for such needs! Frequently it took persuasive perseverance on the part of his concerned family to get him to emerge, oily and dirty, just long enough to eat a hasty meal.

Fourteen-year old Danny, tall, blond, good looking, with his mom's smile and a mischievous twinkle in his eyes, had his dad's genius for repair. His specialty was bicycles. Those nationals fortunate enough to own such a vehicle knew where to bring it when there was need. Like his father, Danny never seemed to lack customers.

Sixteen-year old Becky greeted me with a welcome-home bear hug. Of average height, smiling, with long wavy hair parted in the middle, simply but attractively dressed in clothes which she herself had made, Becky seemed ready for most anything. In an emergency she could jump on the Honda and be off in a cloud of dust to commandeer the national nurse for a neighbor woman in labor. Just as efficiently she could prepare delicious salads of bananas, mangos, papaya, pineapple, oranges and other tropical fruits topped with homemade yogurt. In the kitchen Mayaya the cook was her willing slave. On occasions, on bright moonlight nights he joined Danny and Becky on a hunting expedition to supply meat for the table.

An enormous beetle desperately swinging from a string in the doorway was destined shortly to become part of the unusual Beetle Collection. The pet monkey scolded and chattered for attention whenever Becky passed his cage to go to the tent erected in the shade of the spreading mango tree in the back yard. There she and Mustafo, the faithful Shepherd dog, made their headquarters during our stay. Her own bedroom was turned over to Katie while Danny cheerfully disoccupied his den for me.

Unassumingly Winnie kept the household running smoothly. To meet the limited budget she planned tasty, balanced meals using native foods whenever possible, supplimented by precious dry-season vegetables from the garden and home canned meats such as chicken, rabbit, antelope and even beef. She was ever mindful of the needs of the nationals, physical as well as spiritual, administering food and clothing and comfort, especially to those of the "household of faith."

In their busy life of service the Grings Family exemplified the admonition of the Lord Jesus: "Whosoever will be great among you, let him be your servant" and again "We are your servants for Jesus' sake."

"Aunt K." and Danny immediately took a liking to each other. Katie had hoped to be of some use on the station during her visit. Here was her "charge," a boy who needed to get at his math. Many an afternoon or evening she "rang the school bell" and a reluctant Danny dutifully came in from outdoor fun and repair to wrestle with fractions and algebra. Reward proved worth the drudgery. In just three weeks he was able to complete the whole semester's course and his tests came back from the States with high grades.

After a few days of orienting Katie to a primitive but wholesome way of life and re-orienting myself to the Kituba language, highest on the agenda was a trip to Mangungu, my former home and Irene's burial place. Winnie and Becky worked late Saturday night and rose early Sunday morning to prepare food and supplies for the all-day trip while Dan and his dad rechecked the old Jeep and its tires and packed traveling paraphernalia and burlap bags of manioc. The manioc is the Zairian staple and was taken along to give to the Christians.

There was the usual lineup of nationals who begged to go along, and as many as possible were crowded into the back of the truck along with the rest of the Grings family. As honored guests Katie and I sat with the driver. We didn't mind straddling the big battery on the floor. We knew that if that battery weren't being charged by the Jeep motor as we drove, there was no means of providing electrical energy for the two-way radio, the only means of emergency communication with other stations in Zaire.

We took the back way through the grasslands thus bypassing Kimpata village where I and my well-meaning rescuers had been ambushed by the *Jeunesse* on our way to the Idiofa airport. It was familiar territory and absorbed in my own thoughts I was scarcely aware of the bumpy road. With Bob at the wheel I felt safe and at ease. We would be arriving unannounced and unexpected. Whom would I see? How would they react? Might they not be resentful because of the sufferings which had come upon them for befriending me? My heart beat faster as we neared our destination.

Now we were entering Luembe, Pastor Zechariah's parish. Informed that all of the Christians from both local churches and most of the village folk were at a baptismal service, we set out for the river. The meeting had just been dismissed and people were already swarming up the bank. Several recognized me and stopped dead in their tracks, staring in amazement. "Mama Hege!" "Matonda Nzambi!" (Thank God) Word of our presence passed quickly from mouth to mouth. Some laughed, some cried, others just stood and gazed in unbelief. I was to them as one raised from the dead. One little old lady grabbed me by the shoulders and danced me around, chanting, "Mama Hege is back! Matonda!"

I was eagerly searching the throng for the faces I most longed to see. Suddenly I saw Pastor Luka hurrying toward me. "Thank God, my eyes are seeing you again." Over and over the words spilled out. Quiet tears ran down his cheeks as he held both my hands in his. My eyes were wet too.

Close behind him came Pastor Zechariah, my faithful bodyguard who during those four perilous days had repeatedly risked his life to spare mine. Deeply moved he exclaimed, "I did not think my eyes would see you again this side of heaven. God is good!" "Yes God is good!" I echoed as I looked into those dear faces, the same I had known before, only now they were furrowed with marks which spoke eloquently of suffering and hardships during the intervening years.

In the midst of a growing circle of excitedly chattering friends we made our way back up the hill to the chapel. When called upon to speak in the service which followed I was gratefully surprised at the ease with which the Kituba came back to me. I used Philippians, chapter one with special emphasis on verse 12: "I would ye should understand, brethren, that the things which happened unto me have fallen out rather unto the furtherance of the Gospel." For them as well as for me this was proving true.

After the meeting there were more welcomes, more handshakes, more exclamations, more thanksgiving until we finally broke away from our well-wishers and headed for Mangungu Station in the Jeep.

It was far past noon and I felt emotionally drained, so welcomed the lull. We refreshed ourselves with cold lemonade from the thermos and feasted on home-made peanut butter and jelly sandwiches. Then Winnie spread blankets on the floor and we relaxed in comparative privacy. We were in *my* house, now a far cry from the former cozy home! The tin roof had been taken by the rebels and the villagers had replaced it with palm-leaf thatch. Though used for a school house there was no furniture, neither doors nor windows so it was as freely accessible to the roaming village pigs and chickens as it was to the students.

After a brief rest I stepped outside to further explore the station. Walking to the very spot where Irene and I had fallen together, I stopped and looked over to the palm trees where we had been laid out side by side, both supposedly dead. Winnie, my adoptive sister, came to stand beside me. With feelings too deep for words, each occupied with her own memories, we lingered there for I don't know how long in silence. Then wistfully and slowly, together we followed the path to Irene's grave. The simple cement marker inscribed with John 15:13, "Greater love hath no man than this, that a man lay down his life for his friends", bore mute testimony to her life verse: "Therefore have I set my face like a flint, and I know that I shall not be ashamed" (Isaiah 50:7). Again I was reminded that to Irene was given the great privilege of gaining the martyr's crown. Already she had heard God's "Welcome home, thou good and faithful servant." These were solemn moments of reconsecration — a fresh yielding to the Lord to work out His perfect plan and purpose in what years were left to me. My prayer was:

> Long as I live, Show me Thy way.
> Wherever I may be, Show me Thy way.
> Until life's race is done,
> Until life's battles won,
> Until my crown I've won,
> Show me Thy way.

Painful reminders of the rebellion were everywhere in evidence. The other missionary house on the station was in complete ruins, as were so many houses we visited later. It was not only roofless, but grasses and weeds grew through the cracked cement floors and broken walls. With national helpers, missionaries had labored hard to build adequate housing for their families from the local stones and cement. But as I stood looking at the ruins, there was nothing, not even a window frame to salvage. Everywhere I turned there were marks of great poverty. An extended drought brought the crops to utter failure.

Hunger, malnutrition and sickness were apparent and made me sad.

Arrangements were made for Luka and Zechariah to spend the following Saturday at Kifwanzondo. They arrived early on their bicycles, having left their villages before dawn. There was ample time to visit and reminisce. I asked them to tell me the story of what happened after I left. Both had suffered greatly at the hands of the guerillas. They showed me the scars on their arms and legs, a result of cruel torture. Again I marveled at God's perfect timing when Luka related that early in the morning after my late afternoon rescue by UN helicopter, Mulele Pierre, the communist trained leader of the *Jeusesse*, summoned Luka and me to appear before him. Luka had no choice. He went the two-day journey on foot through jungle paths, without water or food. He said, "I thanked God that you were no longer here to answer the summons for you would have died on the way." Even for this our God would have provided, but in His love and compassion I was rescued on time to be spared all the suffering ahead. Of course, Mulele was annoyed with Luka for letting me escape.

One of the terrorists favorite sports was to tie up their victim in what they scoffingly termed the "Helicopter." With strong, stiff cords the arms were tied behind the back forcing the elbows together. Then the feet were bound, pulled up, and tied to the elbows, thus stretching every muscle and sinew, bending the body backwards with excruciating pain. Often in this position the tormentors hoisted the wretched sufferer and swung him from the limb of a tree while below they scoffed and mocked at his anguish. This they did to Zechariah and started building a fire under him to add to his pain. It was through the intercession of friends that he was released.

Thus tied, Luka was thrown into a pit, face down, to be buried alive because he was accused of hiding a trunk full of money and valuables which he was supposed to have gotten from me. All of our possessions had been confiscated or demolished by the guerillas on the night of the initial attack so there was obviously no such trunk.

Providentially both pastors escaped, and with their families fled into the forest, together with most of the village folks, and there they remained until government troops finally put down the rebellion and brought them out. Hunger and disease claimed the lives of many and those Zairian forests will doubtless witness the opening of many graves on that glorious Resurrection Day.

But all the pursuit and punishment was past as I talked with the two pastors and their lips had only praise to God for His miraculous deliverance. Is it not always so in the lives of God's dear children? The sufferings, mistreatment and anguish are swallowed up in the glories of God's loving presence and comfort. "To them it is given not only to believe on Him but also to suffer for His name's sake." Like sturdy oaks, they had indeed been lashed and beaten by the winds of adversity, but they had not been defeated. Instead the roots of their faith had been driven more deeply into God's unchanging love and faithfulness.

On our second and planned visit to Mangungu, Pastor Luka called the village people together with his "talking drum," a hollowed out log about two feet in diameter. The little preacher took the heavy wooden sticks tipped with crude rubber and skillfully beat the log for about ten minutes. As the rhythmic consonant tones sounded forth, the people began to respond. The new church building, crudely constructed of rock, clay and thatch and open on three sides, was filling to capacity. All the backless log benches were crowded with Pastor Luka's flock as well as with neighboring Pastor Zechariah's people. White visitors, as honored guests, were seated comfortably at the front on kitchen chairs.

We could see that the forthcoming program was generating a great deal of excitement. The music director was a dapper young man dressed in wide bellbottoms, white shirt, and blue scarf looped at his neck because Mobutu permits no men's neckties. He led the young men's double quartet with the confidence of a famous symphony conductor. Using no printed music, not even in practice, they sang in three different languages in almost perfect harmony. At first it was pure delight to relax and listen, but appreciation began to wane a bit after the eighth number, each of which must have had eight stanzas. We were still bravely smiling at the end of the fifteenth song, when fortunately it was time to get on with the rest of the program.

Young Nkedi, the cheerful one, still in charge of primary school and wholly dedicated to his pupils, read a paper on behalf of the local church of Mangungu. It stated how we had labored and suffered together to bring the Gospel to their tribe until I was so suddenly and unexpectedly removed. Then there was an expression of gratitude for my visit and a formal request that I remain and work with them again. As guest speaker, I was asked to bring the morning message. As I watched their familiar faces, so receptive, it would have been easy to yield to their plea to stay, but I knew God had different plans for me.

Other amenities concluded the three-hour service, but after the benediction a lengthy receiving line formed outside the chapel and kept us engaged for another hour. We were glad for relief and time to eat Winnie's savory lunch in the privacy of Pastor Luka's house. We enjoyed an added surprise for even in their abject poverty the Mangungu church contributed a chicken which Luka's wife prepared for us with palm oil and hot seasonings. We invited Luka and his family to join us, but all were too shy except the pastor. Katie was slightly aghast to see him drop his chicken bones on the mud floor, but when she was informed that a village dog would gladly carry them out, she conceded to the convenience of this Zairian custom!

* * * * * * *

We took one long, overnight trip to another tribe to Bwembi, Pastor Mondongo's village. This tall greying man, towering above his people spiritually as well as physically, is a remarkable combination of strength and gentleness. He has a true pastor's heart. He served faithfully with the Eichers as shepherd of the flock at Balaka station until after the rebellion. Then younger carnal Christians, seeking power and personal gain, forced him out of the church. Without bitterness or retaliation he returned to his own village to lead the church there.

We were hospitably received and treated as royal guests in Mondongo's own mud and pole house, though we arrived unannounced. Katie and I were assigned to the best bedroom where we spread our bedrolls over the bamboo mats on the pole beds and fastened our mosquito netting to cross-beam poles above. The fellowship, as we worshiped with the Christians the next morning, in the crowded chapel was sweet and refreshing. We left them, loaded with gifts of pineapple, eggs (presented one at a time, some fresh, some not so fresh, some hard boiled), bananas, and six live chickens which had to be carried in a mesh bag tied to the outside of the Jeep.

Because exams were over, Ruthie Yost had made the trip with us for a last farewell to the people. Her popularity was apparent as several of her former students crowded around her to heartily shake her hand. They were young men with families, whose wives had sacrificed so that they might receive a secondary education to enable them to better serve the Lord as they returned to minister to their own people.

On our way back to Kifwanzondo Bob suggested we make another overnight stop at Hebron, the bombed out missionary rest home. This time we made our beds on the floor of an empty building. We visited the local tribe who showed us how to weave with raffia which was made by stripping a particular kind of palm leaf. We swam in the lake, watched the smoky fires, far off, burning the stubble on harvested fields and felt the closeness of God in the quiet of the night.

At Kifwanzondo I met and thanked the bicycle man who delivered me to the helicopter. He was now a policeman at a nearby village, still unsaved, but he came to pay his respects when word of my visit reached him. There was opportunity again to thank Paka for carrying my urgent, life saving note to the Hallers. Also gratifying were the conversations with the friends at Mangungu, including Chief Nzadi, still personable and still faithful to his commitment to Christ. He was easily picked out of the crowd by his special regalia, wide copper bracelet, loin cloth, and little red beret trimmed with a patch of monkey fur. These set him apart from the rest of the tribe.

My allotted month was just about to end. Three days prior to our scheduled flight to Switzerland for a visit with the Eichers, we drove to Kikwit, the place of the Missionary Rest House and our point of debarkation. There again word of our presence was broadcast. Our visits there were delightful as we met with Zabalon, a former Bible school student now pastoring a church in Kikwit, with dear Timothy, our faithful houseboy, and Gaston, the first nurse who dressed my wound and who was still practicing his profession in the city.

As always it was difficult to say goodbye, so we kept busy making tapes for the Eichers, counseling and encouraging the believers, visiting the big outdoor market at Kikwit, and shopping for the beautiful wax-printed materials the Zairian women drape about their waists for skirts. In contrast to our American styles, any national woman in Zaire who wears a skirt above the ankle is subject to a jail sentence! The pieces of material used for skirts are all the same length. They need no sewing nor ironing and in the hands of the Zairian woman are extremely versatile. Folded into a triangle they are used to fashion original, attractive kitambalas (headdresses). Each woman creates her own style. The skirt is practical for toting the baby on a mother's back, carrying the native lunch when one must travel, serving as a shawl or making a bed cover at night if the owner is cold. We envied the slender stateliness of the Zairian women who unwittingly had achieved the gracefulness of fashion models merely by carrying loads of water, wash, firewood, manioc, and vegetables on their heads.

The four Grings drove with us to the airport at Kikwit. Christian nationals also came to bid farewell. Though the temperature was in the 90's no one seemed impatient when the plane was slow in coming. It was not unusually late by Zairian standards since it was only six hours this time. It is not unheard of to have twelve to twenty-four hour delays!

Perhaps Danny Grings' last request to us best expresses the urgency felt by that depleted little band of faithful workers, "Tell Uncle August (Eicher) to keep the tapes coming!"

* * * * * *

"You will be going as a goodwill ambassador," said the Letter received from Baptist Mid-Missions just before I left the States. We had done our best to fulfill that assignment.

As we taxied down the runway on the hot, stuffy, crowded plane, I felt exhausted, but anything but discouraged. There was a deep sense of gratitude to the Lord for the privilege of returning to my beloved African brethren and for a MISSION ACCOMPLISHED. The national church was aware of our sincere love and concern now, if they were not aware of this fact before our visit. They recognized our oneness with them in their spiritual struggles, material hardships, and physical sufferings.

Arriving in Oron-la-Ville, we spent two weeks in the affectionate hospitality of the Eichers' high-ceilinged and charming old Swiss home. There was a special satisfaction in delivering *maboko ya mono* (with my own hands) letters and tapes from their spiritual children left in Zaire.

This was my first meeting with the Eichers since the rebellion and they had much to recount of God's faithfulness during their ten terrifying days of hiding in the forest before their miraculous rescue. They did not forget to relate His loving kindness during the nine and a half intervening years.

We spent many hours traveling together in the little Austin chauffered by a good friend of the Eichers, Brother Chollet. Mr. Chollet is a retired farmer who beamed with provincial pride as he showed the American visitors the beauties of his native land — Lake Geneva, the Juras, the Alps, and up to Zermatt at the foot of the majestic Matterhorn.

Katie and I were especially gratified to visit the Schaeffers' L'Abri (shelter) of which we had heard and read so much. There scores of young, seeking, disconsolate intellectuals from all nations have found a refuge and have come to the end of their restless search by accepting peace and satisfaction by faith in Jesus Christ.

Zaire — Switzerland — home again. The plane touched down at the Hopkins Airport in Cleveland where our faithful families greeted us with a huge WELCOME HOME sign. We were gratefully aware that every contact during our forty-five day trip was arranged by our almighty, sovereign God. The desire to see my Zairian companions once again, was fulfilled far above my greatest expectations. Our next meeting will doubtless be in our Saviour's presence when we join the chorus of all the redeemed from every kindred and tribe and tongue, to sing praises "unto Him who loved us and washed us from our sins in His own blood."